Alienation:
An Introduction to Marx's Theory

Dan Swain

About the author

Dan Swain is a postgraduate researcher in philosophy at the University of Essex. He is on the editorial board of *International Socialism*, a quarterly journal of socialist theory.

Alienation:
An Introduction to Marx's Theory

Dan Swain

Alienation: An Introduction to Marx's Theory
Dan Swain
First published in January 2012 by Bookmarks Publications
c/o 1 Bloomsbury Street, London WC1B 3QE
© Bookmarks Publications
Cover designed by Esther Neslen
Typeset by Bookmarks Publications
Printed by Russell Press
ISBN 978 1 9051 9299 2

Contents

Acknowledgements

Some of the content for this book is based on my MA dissertation which was completed at the University of Essex and was supervised by Fabian Freyenhagen, who also offered helpful comments on an early draft. Joseph Choonara and Paul Blackledge gave me extremely helpful comments, which I hope I have done some justice to. Thanks also to Sally Campbell at Bookmarks for help throughout the process. Finally, thank you to Julita Skotarska.

Introduction

Let me right at the outset define what I mean by alienation. It is the cry of men who feel themselves the victims of blind economic forces beyond their control. It's the frustration of ordinary people excluded from the processes of decision-making. The feeling of despair and hopelessness that pervades people who feel with justification that they have no real say in shaping or determining their own destinies.[1]

These are the words of Jimmy Reid, the Clydeside trade unionist, after being elected Rector of Glasgow University. In this speech he described and condemned the lived experience of millions of people, and indicated that alienation is much more than just a philosophical concept: "Many may not have rationalised it, may not even understand, may not be able to articulate it. But they feel it".[2]

The young German radical Karl Marx began to diagnose this condition of alienation in the early 1840s, and remained preoccupied with it throughout his life. The theory of alienation he developed described how our human activity could come to be experienced as something external, alien and hostile to us, and the negative effects that could have for our body and mind. Marx saw this experience of alienation not as an inevitable part of the human condition, but as connected to particular ways of organising human activity. The kind of alienation he described was a consequence of an economic system which was then in its infancy, but now dominates the globe: capitalism.

While this book was being written riots broke out across Britain. Beginning in north London following the police killing of Mark Duggan, they spread across the country to other major cities. Many things lay behind these riots, most significantly anger at police repression and racism, but it is no coincidence that they emerged in some of the poorest and most disadvantaged areas of Britain. The people involved in these riots were among the most alienated in the country, people who were more likely to be stopped and searched by the police than to get a job interview. One witness to the riots observed, "This is about as empowered as many of these lads will ever feel. That's the real tragedy".[3] The riots showed the continuing relevance of Marx's ideas about alienation. The howl of rage from people who feel they have no control and no future was visible for anyone who wanted to look.

One of the most striking stories during the riots was an interview conducted by a BBC journalist with two young women. The BBC, typically, sought to portray them as criminal, feral and ignorant, and presented them with a slightly mocking tone. However, listening to the words they said revealed a deep social alienation. When asked why they were rioting they said:

> It's the government's fault...the Conservatives... It's not even a riot, we're just showing the police we can do what we want, and now we have... It's the rich people, the people who have got businesses, and that's why all of this has happened, because of the rich people. It's about showing the rich people we do what we want.[4]

For these women, and hundreds of thousands like them, brief moments of challenging the police and the rich are the closest to exerting control over their lives they are likely to get. The great tragedy of these words is that these women cannot "do what they want". They are constrained by unemployment, deprivation and poverty, as well as police harassment and racism.

The purpose of this book is to offer an introduction to Marx's theory of alienation, its origins and its continued relevance. As long as we still live under the system Marx analysed, Marx remains relevant. It's worth noting, however, that to refer to a "theory of alienation" in Marx can be a little misleading. Marx does not offer a clear, unambiguous definition of what he means by alienation. Instead we find a theme running through Marx's work which involves describing and diagnosing the connections between the system of capitalist production and the profound social, physical and mental ills that it creates (though even the argument that there is this continuity is controversial, as I will point out in a later chapter). Underlying this is the sense of a system out of control and of our own activity experienced as hostile to us. This, in the broadest sense, is what is meant by alienation.

There is a difficulty in writing about alienation in Marx. For Marx alienation was a complicated phenomenon which permeates every aspect of human life. It has to be examined from a number of different sides and in a number of different ways. Thus, while it is possible to talk about "alienation from labour" and "alienation from others", these are often overlapping and interconnected. It is not easy to chop things into pieces and say, "This is an example of alienation from self; that is a result of alienation from others." So, while this book is divided into chapters on different aspects of alienation, I have also tried to emphasise how interconnected each of these aspects are.

The key thing to remember about Marx's theory of alienation is that it is the concept by which he linked a variety of different social phenomena to show their roots in the capitalist system. As Bertell Ollman puts it, "Alienation is the intellectual construct in which Marx displays the devastating effect of capitalist production on human beings, on their physical and mental states and on the social processes of which they are a part".[5] Marx's concepts are intended to help us understand the world in order to change it, and this book sees Marxism as an activist tradition, not just an academic one. In 1844 Marx wrote that "to be radical is to grasp things by the root"[6]—to be genuinely radical is to try to understand the causes of the ills of our world, so that we can uproot them, and abolish them forever.

Chapter 1

Alienation and Enlightenment

Marx did not develop his ideas about alienation in a vacuum. They have their roots in much of the political and philosophical debate of the Enlightenment and the years that followed it. This was a time characterised by increasing attempts to challenge the divine rule of kings, and pose the question of how society might be organised differently. This period saw a growing capitalist class rebelling against the backward, aristocratic feudalism which restricted their rights and, just as importantly, their ability to make profit. Radical philosophers and thinkers began to examine questions of political legitimacy: when is it legitimate for some people to rule over others?

A crucial part of this was the growth of what would now be called the social sciences, albeit in a far cruder form than what exists today. Broadly, the idea was that in order to determine the way in which human societies ought to be organised they had to understand human nature, and to examine the basic laws governing human behaviour. Human beings ought to, if possible, live according to their nature. If living according to their nature was impossible, then certain constraints could be enforced. For example, the 17th century English political theorist Robert Filmer used these kinds of arguments to justify the rule of kings, arguing that this was simply a re-creation of the natural authority of fatherhood, and that kings were the descendants of Adam, "the first father". His contemporary Thomas Hobbes argued that people's naturally hostile and competitive nature required the authority of a strong and ultimately all-powerful monarch for protection. For others in the Enlightenment, however, these arguments were increasingly turned to more radical conclusions.

The growth of political economy was important among these new ideas. Although these thinkers set the stage for modern economics, their concerns were much wider. Contemporary economics tends to ignore social and political dimensions, whereas these thinkers took them seriously, attempting to offer, as the title of Adam Smith's most famous work suggests, "an inquiry into the nature and causes of the wealth of nations". Smith argued that human beings had a natural "propensity to truck, barter, and exchange one thing for another",[7] which gave rise inevitably to the division of labour to some people doing one kind of work and others doing another. This view of human nature is one that is remarkably resilient today, and it is one that emphasises the importance of individual exchange, and therefore of individual property rights.

This emphasis on individual property rights certainly suited the growing bourgeoisie. For the bourgeoisie it was important to be able to *own* property, but it was just as important to be able to *sell* property. It is worth noting that this is one of the earliest senses in which the word "alienation" occurs. Alienation was commonly used in writings on political economy to mean sale or transfer. This is the sense in which, for example, the American Declaration of Independence talks about "unalienable rights"—rights that cannot be transferred away to someone else. However, when it came to property, early political economists largely treated alienation in this sense as a positive thing which ought to be extended. As capitalism began to come into conflict with the old feudal order, the question of what things could be "alienated", ie sold as property, became crucial. Smith wrote about feudalism holding back the "spirit of capitalism" because "the

Alienation

bourgeois cannot alienate the things of the community without the permission of the king".[8]

An important successor to Adam Smith was David Ricardo. Ricardo developed the project of political economy further, in particular developing what has become known as the labour theory of value. This was a contribution to an argument about the source of the value of particular commodities. Smith had seen the value of commodities as being a combination of the various factors which went into producing them—machinery, rent and so forth. Ricardo argued that it was in fact *labour* which was the important source of value. The value of a commodity is set by the amount of labour that is required to produce it.

This had two important consequences. Firstly, it meant that there was an antagonistic relationship between capitalists and workers. For capitalists to make profit, they had to pay workers less than the value that their labour produced. Secondly, it meant that different commodities could be understood as "embodying" certain quantities of human labour. In producing commodities workers put their labour into an object, and thus externalise it, place it outside of themselves. This notion becomes important for Marx's arguments about alienation, as I will discuss in future chapters.

It is worth noting that the sense of alienation employed by the political economists directly informed Marx's more developed theory. These economists were a huge influence on Marx, and much of his life was spent developing, expanding and criticising their ideas. The influence of this sense of alienation can be seen in some of Marx's earliest writings, for example in his 1844 essay "On the Jewish Question", in which he notes that "selling is the practice of alienation".[9] Here he is consciously playing on various senses of alienation: selling something involves literally transferring it away; the production and sale of a commodity involves the embodying and externalising of human labour; and, finally, certain forms of economic activity are the root of alienation in the broader sense of not feeling at home in the world.

Another important political theorist of the Enlightenment is the French philosopher Jean-Jacques Rousseau, who wrote a number of radical essays criticising the established order in the 18th century. Rousseau's ideas were motivated by a radical critique of the right of kings to rule, but also by a deep suspicion of the transformations going on around him. He witnessed the growth of cities and the ensuing poverty and deprivation alongside enormous wealth, and asked the question, "Is this really progress?"

Rousseau entered an essay-writing competition to answer the question, "Has the restoration of the sciences and arts contributed to the purification of morals?" In other words, had the great strides made in scientific understanding and technology improved the condition of humans? Rousseau's radical answer was not just that it had not, but that it had made things worse. Culture, science and technology had corrupted humankind. He rejected the idea that human beings were selfish or aggressive by nature. Rather, "Man is naturally good, and it is only through their institutions that men become bad".[10] There are two radical insights here. Firstly, that technological progress did not automatically bring about improvement in human life, but also brought misery and suffering. Secondly, that the vast range of "moral" problems in society—people's selfishness and greed, as well as their suffering and unhappiness—are a result of their social institutions, not anything "natural".

Rousseau's work began as a criticism of science, technology and high culture, but he quickly broadened to study the inequality among people. He moved from blaming science and culture to blaming inequality for society's problems: "The first source of evil is inequality; from inequality arose

Alienation

riches... From riches are born luxury and idleness; from luxury arose fine arts, and from idleness the sciences".[11] Rousseau saw political institutions as separating human beings from a "state of nature". This was not Hobbes's state of "war of all against all", but a condition of natural equality in which humans were happy and fulfilled:

> I see an animal less strong than some, less agile than others, but, all things considered the most advantageously organised of all: I see him sating his hunger beneath an oak, slaking his thirst at the first stream, finding his bed at the foot of the same tree that supplied his meal, and with that his needs are satisfied.[12]

However, as humans become organised into societies so as to survive, they develop a sort of pride and vanity (*amour propre*). Their need to be recognised and acknowledged within society leads to hierarchies and eventually divisions.

There is a great deal of debate about how much Rousseau's arguments about the state of nature and the development of human societies are supposed to be understood as a genuine historical story, or merely as a theoretical construction about human nature. However, this is less significant than the thought that there is something about modern society which persistently denies human nature. People in modern society are separated from the natural conditions in which they might be happy and fulfilled, and as a consequence social problems develop.

However, Rousseau saw this as a general feature of human society. Because inequality was rooted in the vanity and pride caused by living in societies, it could not be avoided. This was partly because for Rousseau human beings were not naturally social animals—after all, his description of man in nature quoted above was a strikingly solitary one. This meant that for humans living in societies it was necessary to make agreements which restricted the effect of these inequalities. This is Rousseau's famous "social contract".

The social contract itself was nothing new, but Rousseau's formulation was different from others' (John Locke's, for example). Previous social contract theories tended to argue that people should only agree to give certain powers to the state that are necessary for the common good. Most of their rights, especially to property, they retained for themselves. Rousseau, however, argued that this was impossible. Since there were no rights in the state of nature, rights could come about only through social convention in the social contract. Individuals therefore had to give themselves up *entirely* to the community or state. Using broadly the same sense of alienation as the political economists, Rousseau described this as "the total alienation of each associate, together with all his rights, to the whole community".[13]

The state, then, was founded on each individual alienating themselves, their rights and their individual liberty. This can be seen as a reaction against the idea of "universal saleability" promoted by some economists. Rousseau argued that it was not legitimate to alienate away certain kinds of liberty *except* to the state:

> To alienate is to give or to sell...but for what does a people sell itself?... Even if each man could alienate himself, he could not alienate his children: they are born man and free; their liberty belongs to them, and no one but they has the right to dispose of it.[14]

Thus you could not agree to put yourself into slavery, for example. The solution, however, was *collective* alienation, where everyone gave up everything to the community.

Rousseau did not, however, argue against private property or individual liberty. He thought that this act of collective alienation was necessary precisely to *safeguard* private

Alienation

property, to make its concept meaningful. He wrote that the principle of private property was "the most sacred of all the rights of citizenship, and even more important in some respects than liberty itself".[15] Property, and liberty, meant nothing if they did not exist within a society which recognised them and gave them legitimacy.

Much of Rousseau's work can undoubtedly be seen as an early reaction to the conditions of capitalism, its degrading effect on working people, and its gross inequalities. However, the radicalism of his critique was blunted by an inability to see beyond the structures of capitalism itself, and by an account of human nature which was pessimistic about the ability of humans to coexist socially.

Chapter 2

Hegel, Feuerbach and Marx

By the time Marx was a student the thinkers of the Enlightenment had given way to another towering figure of Western philosophy, GWF Hegel. Hegel's ideas and system dominated the philosophical scene, and most people framed their arguments within the terms set by Hegel's work. Broadly, these could be divided into two camps, with the Right Hegelians emphasising Hegel's more conservative aspects, and the Left Hegelians emphasising the more radical possibilities of his system. Marx, along with Friedrich Engels, who was to become a lifetime collaborator, found himself among the Left Hegelians, young radicals who attacked the repressive Prussian monarchy.

A crucial feature of Hegel's philosophy had been his attempts to develop a philosophy of history. It's easy to understand why this was. He had lived through the period beginning with the French Revolution and culminating with the Napoleonic Wars. Europe underwent enormous turmoil and transformation, and it became of huge importance to grasp that transformation as part of a historical process. Hegel saw history as first and foremost the history of human freedom. An important feature of Hegel's theory is the way in which it describes how certain stages in human history are superseded by others. Hegel saw stages in the history of humanity as temporary, and containing tendencies towards each being overcome and replaced by a new, higher, and better stage. This was a major advance on theories such as those of Rousseau which tended to see a simple division between "civilisation" and a "state of nature", with no sense that it might be possible to overcome conflicts in a new form of society rather than go back.

For Hegel, human spirit was free, but it did not always recognise itself as such. The process of history was the process of humans coming to recognise themselves as free. Different social formations offered different possibilities for this kind of recognition, and each successive historical stage came closer to this realisation. For Hegel, Napoleon embodied the spirit of the French Revolution and thus was the human embodiment of this freedom marching across Europe.

Hegel had a very particular conception of freedom, however, which was based on an understanding of freedom as *self-realisation*. Freedom was not merely about removing obstacles to our liberty, but about actively coming to recognise ourselves in the world. The contemporary philosopher Charles Taylor calls this way of thinking about freedom "expressivism":

> Man comes to know himself by expressing and hence clarifying what he is and recognising himself in this expression. The specific property of human life is to culminate in self-awareness through expression.[16]

On this view it is through expressing themselves creatively in the world that human beings come to understand themselves better, and thus live more fulfilling lives.

For Hegel, however, this freedom was expressed in terms of "spirit", understood partly in religious terms. Human history was a story of humans coming to realise that the world of spirit and the physical world are in fact one and the same thing. Initially the spiritual and the physical are united in an "essential unity". Recognition of the external, material world then separates humans from spirit. This state of *alienation*, where human beings see themselves as something *other* than spirit (alien from it), gradually comes to be corrected through several stages of knowledge. Humans come to recognise themselves as free in the world, restoring this original unity, but at a higher level. Each stage of this gradual process is a stage of alienation, but coming closer to true knowledge.

Crucial to these stages is an account of *externalisation*. We act on the external world, shaping it in certain ways, and in this process we project elements of ourselves onto the outside world, "externalising" them. This is how we can come to recognise ourselves in the world, making the world a part of us, and ourselves a part of the world. The modern state is one example of this, a result of the externalisation of certain human powers into something which exists over and above ordinary people.

However, Hegel's account, because it rested on these ideas about spirit, ultimately resolved these questions only in the realm of thought. The solution to these various inadequate forms of human society was merely to find ourselves "at home in our other-being as such"[17]—essentially to come to an acceptance of our place within society. Furthermore, despite his emphasis on the way in which human history changes, he ended up defending the Prussian constitutional monarchy as the highest possible form of society. Despite developing a philosophical system based on change and transformation, Hegel's history stopped at the 19th century.

Hegel was an idealist. He believed that everything existed as ideas, ultimately in the mind of God. Nonetheless his system set the scene for radical criticism based on *materialism*. The first to do this was German Left Hegelian philosopher Ludwig Feuerbach. Feuerbach criticised Hegel's theory from a standpoint of atheism. He turned Hegel's system upside down. Seeing ourselves as spirit, or coming to know God, was not the solution to alienation, but the *result* of alienation.

Alienation

In his 1841 book *The Essence of Christianity*, Feuerbach argued that religious ideas were merely "alienated" or "externalised" features of human life. Human beings created an image of God as a being with human powers. They project *human* powers, thought, speech, creativity and so on, onto an imaginary divine being. In this way they alienate their own abilities, and devalue them in the process. God is exalted as all-powerful and magnificent, while human beings are seen as powerless, insignificant and irrelevant.

Feuerbach's ideas were hugely significant for Marx and his contemporaries. Feuerbach had reasserted the fact that human activity came before philosophical and religious ideas. It was the way that humans actually lived which determined their ideas, not the grand movement of ideas that determined how they lived. Engels described how:

> With one blow, it pulverised the contradiction [of the Hegelian system], in that without circumlocutions it placed materialism on the throne again. Nature exists independently of all philosophy. It is the foundation upon which we human beings, ourselves products of nature, have grown up. Nothing exists outside nature and man, and the higher beings our religious fantasies have created are only the fantastic reflection of our own essence.[18]

This was a central insight which informed Marx's own account of alienation: The ideas in our heads are a direct consequence of the material conditions in which we live.

However, Feuerbach's arguments were themselves somewhat limited. He lacked any conception of transformation which might remove the conditions that give rise to these ideas. Thus all he offered as a solution was a programme of education. Just as Hegel believed that people had to come to know their nature as *spiritual* beings, Feuerbach argued that they had to know themselves as *material* beings. With this realisation of our true nature the damaging ideas of religion would disappear. People could then lead fulfilling lives, having abandoned the belief that they are governed by a higher power. They would realise that the powers they ascribed to God were in fact their own, and that they were capable of great things.

It was in Marx's criticism of both Hegel and Feuerbach that he developed his own account of alienation. Marx criticised first Hegel's theories, under the influence of Feuerbach, then later Feuerbach himself. Agreeing with Feuerbach's materialism, Marx criticised Hegel for ultimately collapsing his system into idealism. While Hegel was correct to see the importance of the way people come to realise themselves in the world, he had underestimated the material barriers to achieving this realisation. He was guilty of "merely apparent criticism".[19] This is because he had focused mainly on thought, on consciousness, as the way people realise themselves in the world.

Marx argued that it was not thought which was essential to realising ourselves in the world, but conscious productive activity—labour. While Hegel had discussed human activity, it was merely as manifestations of different stages of knowledge. This had left him blind to the real consequences of this activity. In contrast to Hegel's growing acceptance of the political status quo, Marx saw around him great suffering, oppression and unhappiness, and therefore became preoccupied with explaining how people *failed* to realise themselves in their activity:

> What requires explanation is not the *unity* of living and active human beings with the natural, inorganic conditions of their metabolism with nature, and therefore their appropriation of nature; nor is this the result of a historic process. What we must explain is the *separation* of these inorganic

Alienation

conditions of human existence from this active existence, a separation which is only fully completed in the relationship between wage-labour and capital.[20]

Because Hegel had privileged *ideas* above practical human activity, he had failed to see the negative side of the way in which we externalise ourselves in the world.

Much of Marx's criticism of Hegel comes through his reading of Feuerbach. However, Marx and Engels quickly broke with Feuerbach as well. They criticised Feuerbach's focus on education as the solution to the problem of alienation. Feuerbach had, entirely correctly, identified that ideas in our heads are a reflection of our material existence; that, as Marx and Engels later put it, "the phantoms formed in the human brain are also, necessarily, sublimates of their material life-process".[21] However, the solution he had proposed remained entirely at the level of changing people's *ideas*, of educating them to live differently. Marx saw this as profoundly inadequate.

Part of Feuerbach's problem was that he had a static conception of human nature, one that could not change. He saw humans as naturally social beings who ought to live in particular societies in a particular way. All that was required was to educate people about the correct way to live according to this true nature. While this conception was a significant step forward from the individualistic notions of human nature of the Enlightenment, it was also profoundly limited. In denying the idealism of Hegel's system he had also denied its dynamism and radicalism—the idea that human societies are subject to change and can be superseded by new ones.

Marx rejected Feuerbach's static notion of human nature. Instead, he wrote of human nature that "in its reality it is the ensemble of the social relations".[22] By this he meant that it changed according to the different ways in which society was organised. Crucial to this was the different ways in which *labour* was organised. Marx shifted the focus away from a human nature inherent in each individual to the relationship between humans and nature—the way in which people actively work on the external world and realise themselves in it.

If labour plays this central role then two things become of paramount importance: (1) the different means with which people perform their labour (tools, machinery, etc); and (2) the different ways in which labour is organised. Hegel saw the history of different ways of social organisation as different forms of spirit realising itself. For Marx the opposite is true. Different forms of social organisation and different means of production drive forward history, and give rise to different ideas about society. It was not a new stage of the human spirit that had created capitalism, but capitalism that had created the particular experience of humans who lived under it. Different tools and different ways of organising labour allow for different ways of expressing (or failing to express) ourselves through work.

This meant that it was possible to overcome alienation only by transforming the way people organise their labour. Attempts at education to change people's ideas would be futile without simultaneously transforming the conditions in which they lived. In his 1845 "Theses on Feuerbach" Marx wrote:

> The materialist doctrine concerning the changing of circumstances and upbringing forgets that circumstances are changed by men and that it is essential to educate the educator himself. The coincidence of the changing of circumstances and of human activity or self-changing can be conceived and rationally understood only as *revolutionary practice*.[23]

Eradicating the phantoms in people's heads requires transforming the circumstances in which they live and work. And this requires revolutionary practice. These two points, the centrality of labour and the importance of revolutionary transformation, are key to understanding all of Marx's work, particularly his ideas on alienation, and I will return to them in later chapters. For Marx the central question was how we actively transform the world. So the famous claim that "philosophers have only interpreted the world in various ways; the point is to change it"[24] is more than just a call to arms; it is intended as a philosophical revolution.

Chapter 3

A universal class

For Rousseau, Hegel and Feuerbach alienation had been something that was a general human condition. It affected everyone living in a particular society in broadly the same way. Marx, however, observed that some were more alienated than others. Society was divided into different classes, and these classes experienced alienation in different ways:

> The propertied class and the class of the proletariat present the same human self-estrangement. But the former class feels at ease and strengthened in this self-estrangement, it recognises estrangement as its own power and has in it the semblance of a human existence.[25]

The proletariat, the working class under capitalism, experienced alienation far more acutely than their employers.

The growth of the proletariat formed an important part of Marx's analysis. Capitalist production required dividing society into two classes. The first class owned the means of production, ie the machinery, tools and finance required to produce things. The second class had nothing to sell but their ability to labour. Marx later described the worker as free "in a double sense" in that, "as a free individual he can dispose of his labour power as his own commodity, and that on the other hand, he has no other commodity for sale, ie he is rid of them, he is free of all the objects needed for the realisation of his labour power".[26] In other words these people are free to sell their ability to labour (their labour power) for a fixed time—they are not slaves—but at the same time they have no choice but to do so, because they have nothing else to sell.

This class came into existence due to two processes. On the one hand, the industrial revolution created new forms of machinery which required workers to be concentrated in certain workplaces, rather than working from home. This equipment was not owned by the individual worker, but by a capitalist. On the other hand, creating a large group of people to work in the factories required a process of mass expropriation, which Marx called "primitive accumulation". This involved throwing peasants off their land—"those moments when great masses of men are suddenly and forcibly torn from their means of subsistence, and hurled as free and unattached proletarians on the labour-market". Marx described how this took place "under conditions of ruthless terrorism",[27] where communal, church and state-owned lands were seized by individual capitalists. The most severe example of this was the Highland clearances in Scotland, which saw thousands of families driven off their land. Many of these were then later re-employed to work on the land that had once been their home.

For Marx, the proletariat were of enormous political and theoretical importance. One reason for this was their suffering. The largest working class in Europe at that time was to be found in England, where capitalism had taken root earliest. These changes had concentrated workers into massively expanded cities, in conditions of ill-health and misery. In 1845 Engels wrote a study of the working class in England where he described this suffering in close detail. In a typical passage he describes how:

> They are supplied bad, tattered, or rotten clothing, adulterated and indigestible food. They are exposed to the most exciting changes of mental condition, the most

violent vibrations between hope and fear; they are hunted like game, and not permitted to attain peace of mind and quiet enjoyment of life. They are deprived of all enjoyments except that of sexual indulgence and drunkenness, are worked every day to the point of complete exhaustion of their mental and physical energies, and are thus constantly spurred on to the maddest excess in the only two enjoyments at their command.[28]

These conditions were a direct result of the capitalist system, of removing people from the security of the land, forcing them to sell their labour and concentrating them in overcrowded cities.

However, Marx quickly moved on from a concern for the suffering of the working class to realising their radical potential. Marx had become tired of a certain kind of ineffective criticism which was disconnected from real people in society. He argued that for criticism to become truly powerful it must be capable of "gripping the masses". Criticism alone was powerless without some kind of social force to back it up. In addition, he had despaired of the liberal, intellectual bourgeois community he lived in, losing faith that they could ever be a radical force (they lacked the "revolutionary boldness, which flings into the face of the adversary the defiant words: *I am nothing, I should be everything*").[29] Instead, Marx looked to the growing proletariat as the radical force to change society.

The significance of the proletariat lay in their unique position in capitalist society. Unlike any previous class in history they were universally and by necessity dispossessed. The proletariat, by very definition, were separated from the means of producing wealth. They therefore had no vested interest in the system, no property to defend. When the bourgeoisie had overthrown the old feudal society, the result had been a

Alienation

new form of class rule, capitalism, with a new form of property. In contrast, a revolution led by the proletariat would lead to the abolition of class divisions. Marx describes the proletariat as a class which "has a universal character because of its universal suffering". It does not claim any "*particular right* because the wrong it suffers is not a *particular wrong*, but *wrong in general*".[30]

Although at this stage in his life Marx is writing in high-handed philosophical language influenced by Hegel, the important insights here are simple ones. Marx believed that the position of the working class within the capitalist system meant that they were the only class capable of abolishing capitalism completely, and, significantly, the first class in history capable of abolishing class division (and therefore exploitation and alienation) altogether. Unlike any other class of people, the working class have no particular interest in the capitalist system. This means that their struggles can take the form of a struggle against the *entire* system, not just one aspect of it.

Furthermore, the working class have a great deal of power within capitalism. If they stopped working, the system would grind to a halt and the capitalists would be unable to continue to make profits. Furthermore, smaller, specific groups of workers could be exceptionally powerful because of how integrated the economy had become. If, for example, transport workers went on strike, it would not just hurt transport bosses, but many other capitalists as well. The working class were therefore strategically hugely important, more so than other exploited or oppressed groups. Because they were integral to *making* capitalism, they were also integral to *breaking* it.

However, to break capitalism, and even to defend their own interests within capitalism, workers had to act collectively. A strike or other industrial action simply cannot be effective if some people continue to work. A collective decision has to be reached and collective action taken. Marx thought that this distinguished the proletariat from other classes, who were just as much in competition with each other as they were with their bosses. Because they had to act collectively in their struggles, Marx believed that the proletariat would be able to abolish class divisions altogether, and collective cooperation could replace competition. This is why Marx argued that, "however limited an industrial revolt may be, it contains within itself a universal soul".[31]

It is important to stress that Marx's ideas about the proletariat were developed through many years of close study and participation in working class movements. Within months of Marx writing about the theoretical importance of the proletariat in his critique of Hegel, significant events took place which confirmed his analysis. In 1844 weavers in Silesia (then in Prussia, now in Poland) rose up in protest demanding higher wages. This quickly escalated to conflicts with the Prussian state. This was a tremendously significant uprising which had a great influence on many in Prussia. It was something of a watershed moment, in which many of Marx's apparently radical contemporaries failed an important test. For example, Marx's former colleague Arnold Ruge criticised and downplayed the importance of the revolt.

In his writings of this period, written as a criticism of Ruge, Marx observed how the weavers' revolt moved rapidly from economic to social demands, pointing to their "intrepid battle-cry which does not even mention hearth, factory or district but in which the proletariat at once proclaims its antagonism to the society of private property in the most decisive, aggressive, ruthless and forceful manner".[32] He believed it was extremely significant that what had begun as merely a set of economic demands had quickly transformed into a demand for the transformation of society. The supposedly backward, uneducated weavers had developed a criticism of society which went far beyond that of Marx's liberal intellectual friends.

This was a persistent feature of working class revolts throughout Marx's life. The 1844 revolts were an early stage in the process that led to the enormous revolutions and upheavals of 1848. Marx and Engels threw themselves into these revolts, wholeheartedly supporting the democratic demands they involved, but also arguing that only the working class could ultimately realise a genuinely democratic state. Marx and Engels's confidence in the working class is clear enough in the *Communist Manifesto*, written on the eve of these revolutions, where they argue, "The theoretical conclusions of the Communists are not in any way based on ideas or principles that have been invented, or discovered by this or that would-be reformer. They merely express, in general terms, actual relations springing from an existing class struggle, from a historical movement going on under our very eyes".[33]

It's worth noting that Marx and Engels were not the only people to witness this movement. Many theorists of the bourgeoisie saw exactly this potential themselves. The influential political theorist Alexis de Tocqueville, writing from the other side of the barricades in 1848, saw it clearly enough:

> Inevitably they were bound to discover sooner or later that what held them back in their place was not the constitution of the government, but the unalterable laws that constitute society itself; and it was natural for them to ask whether they did not have the power and the right to change these too, as they had changed the others.[34]

Of course, what distinguished Marx from de Tocqueville was that he did not believe that the laws of society were "unalterable" and that he welcomed the workers' challenge to them.

When Marx described the proletariat it was a new and growing group in society. It was a small minority, even in western Europe, and it barely existed across the rest of the world. However, Marx anticipated that capitalism's expansion depended on making more and more workers free in the double sense. Workers would become the overwhelming majority of the population, and this also formed a part of their revolutionary potential:

> All previous historical movements were movements of minorities, or in the interest of minorities. The proletarian movement is the self-conscious, independent movement of the immense majority, in the interest of the immense majority.[35]

This prediction proved to be completely accurate. There is now a vast, global working class, spanning the world. The process of development of the global South has created and continues to create huge groups of people, mostly in cities, who depend for their survival on working for someone else. In the developed world the working class remains enormous as well. They are often materially better off than those in the developing world, but they are still entirely dependent on employment to survive.

In Marx's analysis of the proletariat we can see how he viewed alienation as a double-edged sword. While capitalism brought about universal alienation, suffering and dispossession, it also created the possibility for radical change that had never existed before. Widespread alienation created the conditions and drive towards its own overthrow and supersession. Because of their universal alienation from property Marx saw the proletariat as capable of abolishing class divisions entirely. It was capable of representing all of humanity, being a universal class: "When the proletariat demands the negation of private property, it is only elevating to a principle for society what society has already made a principle for the proletariat".[36]

Chapter 4

Alienation from the labour process

Marx's account of alienation placed human labour at its centre. This was not "human activity" as understood by Hegel
in merely abstract terms, but the concrete, specific ways in
which human beings worked on the world around them. For
Marx, "To say that man is a corporeal, living, real, sensuous,
objective being with natural powers means that he has real,
sensuous objects as the objects of his being and of his vital
expression, or that he can only express his life in *real, sensuous
objects*".[37] In saying this he was arguing that we have to look
to the particular ways in which practical activity is organised
if we want to understand the conditions human beings find
themselves in. It is productive activity, consciously shaping
our environment in creative ways, rather than merely intellectual activity, that is key to realising ourselves in the world.

Marx emphasised the role of labour in a number of ways.
Firstly, the way in which human beings labour is what distinguishes them from animals:

> A spider conducts operations which resemble those of the
> weaver, and a bee would put many a human architect to
> shame by the construction of its honeycomb cells. But what
> distinguished the worst architect from the best of bees is
> that the architect builds the cell in his mind before he con-
> structs it in wax. At the end of every labour process, a result
> emerges which had already been conceived by the worker at
> the beginning, hence already existed ideally.[38]

Human labour is characterised by being a collective, conscious, creative and transforming engagement with the natural world. While the spider and the bee transform their environment to meet their needs, and bees even do so collectively, they act only according to instincts. Humans, on the other hand, plan their labour in advance, and furthermore they can produce *new* and *different* things.

For Marx, labour meant far more than what is narrowly considered work under capitalism. "Work" is often understood as describing only certain kinds of human activity which are "useful" or "productive". Under capitalism, this is generally labour performed by workers for a wage. However, for Marx, labour meant any human activity which involves the collective, creative transformation of the natural world.

This meant that Marx made a significant break from a tradition of talking about labour as a burden, or as necessary but undesirable. Many of the economists Marx was reading, while acknowledging the importance of labour for value, still saw it as something which was essentially burdensome. In contrast Marx saw labour as a vital part of human activity which could be the source of genuine fulfilment and expression. In fact, he attacked these ideas as *themselves* the result of alienation. The fact that we experience work as merely burdensome and feel happier outside of it is because of our alienation from it: "The result is that man (the worker) feels that he is acting freely only in his animal functions—eating, drinking, procreating, or at most in his dwelling and adornment".[39]

An example of this is the distinction between leisure and work which is common in modern society. People perform all sorts of creative activity in their so-called "leisure time"— they make music, build models, play sport, read and write literature, and perform a vast range of other activities. Yet this is seen as merely unproductive leisure activity, or "hobbies", something to be done in between the useful work, to keep us occupied during the time between clocking off and clocking on again. In turn, the "leisure industry" creates a lucrative business on the back of this distinction. It finds all sorts of ways of commodifying and regimenting leisure so as to make profit from it. People's very diverse interests and projects are seen as merely a sideshow to their importance as, on one side, a waged labourer, and on the other, a passive consumer.

In the *Economic and Philosophical Manuscripts* Marx talks about the importance of labour in terms of *species-being*. This is a tricky concept which has caused some controversy, but can broadly be understood as a concept of human nature. However, this is not the vision of human nature promoted by Rousseau or Hobbes, or for that matter *Daily Mail* columnists, in which, for example, we are all "naturally" greedy and women are "naturally" housewives. Nor is it the fixed, static, conception of species-being employed by Feuerbach. Marx shifted the focus away from something inherent in the individual, and onto the relationships between people. Labour was the most fundamental of these relationships. Marx describes the importance of labour as "the everlasting nature-imposed condition of human existence".[40] The one constant fact about humans throughout history is that they labour on the world in collective, conscious and creative ways, firstly to meet immediate needs and then to go beyond those needs: "Conscious life activity distinguishes man immediately from animal life activity".[41] Species-being remains a controversial concept, and some of those controversies will be addressed in Chapter 10.

Labour is first and foremost a collective act. The amount that any one person can achieve on their own is very limited. Only the most basic needs can be met, and often not even those. By contrast, through cooperation incredible things can be achieved. Despite the mythologies of right wing economists and historians, humans have always existed in societies, in which labour has been cooperatively organised. The key question has always been what the terms of that cooperation will be. This means that labour, for Marx, plays a central role in shaping social relationships.

Alienation was, for Marx, about lack of control over our labour. The source of alienation was to be found in the lack of control of workers over the process of production. While this had been the case in all societies where one class dominated another, under capitalism it took a particular form. Because workers do not own means of production, they have to sell their labour power to capitalists to survive. In this way labour power itself becomes a commodity—something to be bought and sold on the market. In selling this commodity workers give over a portion of their time each day to create new value for a capitalist.

It is this process, the transformation of human labour into a commodity, which gives rise to the various dimensions of alienation that Marx analysed. It is the most fundamental form of alienation under capitalism (Marx describes other aspects of alienation as "summarising" alienation from the labour process). In selling their labour power to capitalists workers don't just lose some free time in which they could otherwise have done what they wanted—they lose all control over a vital part of their life: "The activity of the worker is not his spontaneous activity. It belongs to another, it is a loss of his self".[42] Their creative powers are channelled not towards their own projects, but towards the requirements of a boss.

Control is the most significant aspect here. Those who sell their labour power, literally alienating it away, lose all control over it. The labour process becomes something under the control of someone else and ultimately outside of any control whatsoever.

The needs of capitalism as a system mean that people are denied expression through their work. Firstly, capitalist

Alienation

production is organised according to strict structures of authority and command: "That a capitalist should command in the field of production is now as indispensable as that a general should command on the field of battle".[43] Capitalism demands that most workers are not involved in the decision-making related to their jobs. Having sold their time to an employer, the employer can, more or less, tell them how to work and where.

In addition, from the point of view of a capitalist labour is something that has to be made uniform. This is not to say that every job has to be the same, but that it has to be measured in *abstract* terms. It must be countable, measurable, and comparable to other units of labour—it has to be quantifiable. This process of homogenisation cannot avoid transforming work in dramatic ways. Marx describes how workers come to be seen, and also begin to see themselves, as merely "abstract activity and a stomach".[44]

This need for measurement comes from the needs of capitalism itself. Capitalism rests, according to Marx, on treating human activity as abstract labour. Under capitalism all commodities have both a use-value and an exchange-value. As use-values commodities are the product of concrete human labour, possessing a use to humans which is "activated" by social relations, but independent of them. However, commodities are exchanged on the market according to their exchange-value, and to acquire this they must be seen as "merely congealed quantities of homogeneous human labour, ie of human labour power expended without regard to the form of its expenditure".[45] For capitalism to function, for it to be possible to exchange commodities according to certain standards, human labour has to be seen in these abstract terms. As a result, the particular, human quality of the labour of some particular individual becomes subordinated to abstract labour, homogenised and measurable.

Alienation from the labour process

Anyone who has worked in higher education over the past decades will be familiar with the constant demand to quantify and regulate labour and labour time. The arcane, confusing and much hated Research Assessment Exercise is one example of this. As Alex Callinicos describes:

> Academics are employed to engage in research as well as teach (two fifths of their salary is notionally to pay them to do research). How then to measure their productivity? Analogies with industry require that some physical output can be found that can be measured.[46]

Thus the demands of capitalism require that the work of research and teaching be just as measurable and quantifiable as any other kind of work. It has to be possible to compare the work of a lecturer with that of any other worker in an abstract way. Similarly, what is taught has to be measured. Great emphasis is placed on "transferable skills", which students are supposed to learn alongside their other studies. One job advice website describes these as "competencies that can be carried over from one activity to another". It is not hard to see the connection between this and abstract labour, which Marx described as labour "absolutely indifferent to its particular *specificity*, but *capable of all specificities*".[47]

Alienation under capitalism is all the worse because capitalism has unleashed unprecedented possibilities for people to shape the world around them. Previous forms of social production were limited in their creative capacity. In contrast capitalism is a system "whose universality produces not only the alienation of the individual from himself and others but also the universality and the comprehensiveness of his relations and capacities".[48] While the feudal lord had no interest in developing production beyond keeping himself well fed and in charge, capitalists constantly have to compete with one another. Thus they are always forced to look for new, more efficient ways of producing things faster, easier and cheaper. This has the effect of greatly increasing the capacity of humans to shape the world around them, to "realise themselves".

However, this self-realisation is never available to the majority under capitalism. Alongside the creative powers that capitalism unleashes, it brings an even greater denial of those powers, as these productive powers become more and more concentrated in the hands of a small minority, and more and more human activity becomes abstract, homogenised labour. For example, the development of industrial capitalism brought with it entirely new attitudes to time and the regulation of work. Widespread ownership of watches and clocks, and even the inclusion of a minute hand, went hand in hand with the development of wage-labour. Similarly the attempt to control and regiment time became an important concern. Work moved from being irregular, subject to the rhythms of nature and the needs of the particular task, to being constant and measured, working to the whistle instead of until a task is completed. In England capitalists made it a priority to abolish many traditional holidays and festivals, including cracking down on the practice of Saint Mondays—taking Monday off after the weekend—so that more working hours could be squeezed out.[49] All of this contributes to making work seem less fulfilling than it could be.

Modern call centres provide a clear example of this drive to squeeze every possible working minute out of employees. Computerised systems regulate toilet breaks and lunch hours, while strict guidelines dictate exactly how to use your time on the phone most efficiently. Everything is geared towards squeezing every possible minute of labour from workers; the amount of control a worker has over her environment is close to zero. In some call centres workers report being given a flowchart of questions and responses for dealing with customers, so keen are the employers to reduce even this interaction to a mechanical model.

A recent study of call centres in Scotland found that "lack of control over shift patterns was frequently exacerbated by the introduction of new IT arrangements that gave individual employees minimum choice or discretion over shift arrangements",[50] while for many workers "the limitations represented by routinised, intensified and unpredictable work presents a major hurdle in attaining a more fulfilled life".[51] It was not merely rhetoric when civil service union leader Mark Serwotka referred to call centres as "the new dark satanic mills".

In capitalist production workers increasingly seem like mere parts of a grand machine. The Hungarian Marxist philosopher Georg Lukács describes this process well:

> In consequence of the rationalisation of the work-process the human qualities and idiosyncrasies of the worker appear increasingly as mere sources of error when contrasted with these abstract special laws functioning according to rational predictions. Neither objectively nor in his relation to his work does man appear as the authentic master of this process; on the contrary, he is a mechanical part incorporated into a mechanical system. He finds it already pre-existing and self-sufficient, it functions independently of him and he has to conform to its laws whether he likes it or not.[52]

The particular individuality of the worker becomes a barrier to the work process. Individual human characteristics are something to be ironed out and minimised, rather than celebrated or utilised.

Work is broken down into simple monotonous tasks. A British car worker describes work on the production line:

> It's not really skill as such... I mean yeah, you do get a lot of different new things to do, but taken on their own

they're pretty simple jobs. It's not skill, it's like you are really a robot... I can switch off and I'm sitting on a beach in Barbados.[53]

All individuality and creativity is sucked out of this work because of the needs of production: "It's bloody boring".[54]

For Marx, these tendencies were an inevitable consequence of capitalism. Capitalism relies on labour itself being transformed into a commodity, into something that is transferred away into the control of others. This initial alienation is the basis of people being denied expression through their work, and thus has enormous consequences for humanity.

Chapter 5

Alienation from product

Marx also described how under capitalism workers are alienated from the things that they produce. Once again, this has a literal aspect—workers do not own their product, rather it belongs to their employer. Many people work to produce things they will never own themselves—making cars or electrical goods that they could never afford to buy, or serving food in restaurants in which they could never afford to eat. The things which we produce end up as someone else's property; they are never truly ours.

This is as much a feature of modern life as it was in Marx's day. More than one billion people live on less than $1 a day, and more than two billion on $2 a day. Workers in China producing Apple's iPhones earn at most $172 a month—nowhere near enough to buy one of the thousands of fancy gadgets they produce on a daily basis. Nor is it merely a feature of the developing world. Recently the union that represents workers at General Motors in the US pointed out that the workers it represents would find it hard to buy the cars they produce. A major source of protests by migrant workers in America is the sense that they cannot even afford the vegetables that they pick, while many young workers find themselves working for minimum wage or less in restaurants that charge a week's wages for a meal.

The products workers produce are being sold to someone else, by someone else, to make profit for someone else. The idea that we can see them as the products of our creative capacities is completely meaningless. As Marx puts it, "this realisation of labour appears as a *loss of reality* for the worker, objectification as *loss of and bondage to the object*, and appropriation as *estrangement*, as *alienation*".[55] The way we interact with the products we produce becomes completely distorted.

This means that these products, as well as belonging to someone else, appear as something opposed to us: "The life which the worker has conferred on the object confronts him as something hostile and alien".[56] The more energy the worker expends on producing these objects, the less she has of her own: "The more the worker spends himself, the more powerful becomes the alien world of objects which he creates over and against himself, the poorer he himself—his inner world—becomes, the less belongs to him as his own".[57]

The attempts by management to deal with this kind of alienation, to make people believe in and identify with what they produce, are often hilarious. In his account of work at a General Motors truck factory in Michigan, Ben Hamper describes the various techniques management employed. The first was a "quality mascot", Howie Makem, an enormous cat with "a long red cape emblazoned with the letter Q for Quality", who would wander around the plant in a bid to boost morale.[58] The second was a series of neon signs placed around the plant bearing encouraging messages:

> The messages they would flash ranged from corny propaganda (green neon bulb depictions of Howie Makem's face uttering stuff like QUALITY IS THE BACKBONE OF GOOD WORKMANSHIP!) to motivated pep squawk (A WINNER NEVER QUITS & A QUITTER NEVER WINS!) to brain-jarring ruminations (SAFETY IS SAFE)... I remember the first day the message board went into operation. For the entire shift it beamed out one single message...SQUEEZING RIVETS IS FUN![59]

Alienation from product

None of these, perhaps unsurprisingly, seemed to make any noticeable difference to workers' ability to identify with the trucks they were building.

In Chapter 1 I mentioned David Ricardo's argument that labour was the source of value. This meant that the products of human labour were embodiments of that labour, incorporating an aspect of the workers themselves. The machinery that people work on is just as much the product of labour as the things they produce. Thus workers were surrounded by, and dominated by, *embodiments* of their own past labour. Furthermore, Marx described the labour embodied by capital in this way as *dead*. Unlike the "living" labour of the workers, this dead labour—machinery, plant, etc—was unable to create any more value.

Capitalism's constant drive to accumulate more and more leads to this world of dead labour becoming ever bigger. The more work the worker performs, the more of her living labour she pours into this world of dead labour. Yet this world belongs to someone else, and thus appears radically alien. In a famous passage Marx compares capital to a vampire which "only lives by sucking living labour, and lives the more, the more labour it sucks".[60] Descriptions of work often describe the workplace as an independent, hostile living being. In *Germinal*, Emile Zola's 19th century novel about a coal miners' strike in France, he describes how the mine "at the bottom of its hole, with its posture as of an evil beast, continued to crunch, breathing with a heavier and slower respiration, troubled by its painful digestion of human flesh".[61]

While this world of dead objects gets bigger, it does not actually reduce the amount of labour that workers have to perform. While investment in technology and machinery could make workers' lives easier, it tends to just mean new and different kinds of toil. This has been a general story since the development of capitalism. In 1867 a vast trade exposition was held in Paris, showcasing technology from across the world. In *Live Working or Die Fighting* Paul Mason describes how delegates from workers' organisations attended the expo and produced their own reports. Their reaction shocked the authorities: "Instead of a poem of praise to mechanisation the reports read like a sustained critique of the mid-19th century social order".[62] The workers' delegations were not hostile to the new machinery, but saw in it a denial of their own status. This new machinery appeared as symbols of their own worthlessness.

This indicates another feature of alienation under capitalism. Instead of seeing machinery as something which can relieve their burden, as Marx put it, "since the worker has been reduced to a machine, the machine can confront him as a competitor".[63] An extreme example of this can be found in the Luddite movement of the early 19th century, when workers actively destroyed machinery which they saw as a threat to their way of life. The problem still takes a significant form today. The introduction of new technology in a factory or office might signal an improvement in working conditions, but it is just as likely to signal a loss of jobs. Improvements in technology can be, rightly, just as much a cause for fear for workers as a cause for relief.

Chapter 6

Commodity fetishism

Marx's early analysis of alienation laid the foundations for his later, more developed analysis of the capitalist system. Alienation, understood as lack of control over the labour process, had existed in a number of different forms. However, under capitalism, Marx argued, it took a particular form which played an important role in reinforcing and re-creating the system. This form he called commodity fetishism.

Under feudalism, and other forms of society before capitalism, social production was organised in an *immediate* way. The serfs who worked the land gave direct tribute to their feudal lord. This relationship was enforced largely through direct force and coercion. It was the military strength of the lord that allowed him to extract this value. This does not mean that the serfs had control of their labour and their life, far from it. The feudal lord dictated what they did, and production was largely directed towards maintaining his authority and power.

Capitalism is different. It does not rely on the direct appropriation of wealth from one class by another. Rather, it depends on a relationship of exchange on the market. Marx and Engels described this transformation:

> The bourgeoisie, wherever it has got the upper hand, has put an end to all feudal, patriarchal, idyllic relations. It has pitilessly torn asunder the motley feudal ties that bound man to his "natural superiors", and has left remaining no other

nexus between man and man than naked self-interest, than callous "cash payment". It has drowned the most heavenly ecstasies of religious fervour, of chivalrous enthusiasm, of philistine sentimentalism, in the icy water of egotistical calculation. It has resolved personal worth into exchange value, and in place of the numberless indefeasible chartered freedoms, has set up that single, unconscionable freedom— Free Trade.[64]

In the market everyone appears as an independent, autonomous agent who possesses something to exchange, and it is through this process of exchange that capitalism organises itself. It still involves a relationship of exploitation, but it is one which takes place through the apparently free buying and selling of commodities in the marketplace. Workers appear as the owner of a commodity—their own labour in an abstract form—which is bought by a capitalist, who is an owner of capital. As Marx puts it, the capitalist "can undertake the process of exploiting labour only because, being the owner of the conditions of labour power, he confronts the labourer as the owner of only labour power".[65]

People, then, relate to each other not directly, but through *commodities*. This means that relationships between human beings come to look like relationships between objects. This is what Marx meant by *fetishism*: "It is a definite social relation between men, that assumes, in their eyes, the fantastic form of a relation between things".[66] This develops over time, as the capitalist system becomes more established. Each time the process of exchange takes place, the more it seems like an unchanging feature of human life. The social relationships involved in capitalist production begin to crystallise or congeal into objects. Products of labour appear as congealed amounts of abstract labour. Marx describes how in the commodity, "the social character of men's labour appears to them as an objective character stamped upon the product of that labour; because the relation of the producers to the sum total of their own labour is presented to them as a social relation, existing not between themselves, but between the products of their labour".[67]

Marx compares this commodity fetishism to the kind of alienation identified by Feuerbach in religious thought:

> In order, therefore, to find an analogy, we must have recourse to the mist-enveloped regions of the religious world. In that world the productions of the human brain appear as independent beings endowed with life, and entering into relation both with one another and the human race. So it is in the world of commodities with the products of men's hands.[68]

Just as gods come about through projecting human powers into external beings, which then interact with us, send us messages, play tricks on us, etc, in capitalist production commodities appear as independent entities too.

A frequent example of this kind of fetishism is the idea that "money makes money". This is a commonly invoked idea, and from the point of view of the capitalist, it appears to be true. A small stake invested in a business can produce far greater profits. In the short term money can be "grown" without directly investing it, through stock market speculation and so on. Yet, in reality this is merely projecting onto money a property of the natural world. Money does not literally grow in the same way that plants do. Money itself does not produce more wealth. It is the people employed who ultimately produce profit for the investor. Fetishism hides this reality, and suggests that money has some sort of almost mystical expanding power of its own.

The feeling that commodities dominate our lives is an increasingly familiar one. The Canadian activist Naomi

Klein's 2000 book *No Logo* described many of these phenomena, and how advertisers had become expert at manipulating them. For example, she quotes a shoe shop owner describing the way certain products become "must have", and almost become more valuable to people than health or food:

> I do get weary and worn down from it all. I'm always forced to face the fact that I make my money from poor people. A lot of them are on welfare. Sometimes a mother will come in here with a kid, and the kid is dirty and poorly dressed. But the kid wants a hundred-twenty-buck pair of shoes and that stupid mother buys them for him. I can feel that kid's inner need—this desire to own these things and have the feelings that go with them—but it hurts me that this is the way things are.[69]

Klein describes how these brands come to take on a significance way beyond the usefulness of the actual things they sell.

Marx may not have had Nike, Starbucks or Apple to contend with, but he would have recognised some of these features of modern life. He offers the more mundane example of a table:

> The form of wood, for instance, is altered, by making a table out of it. Yet, for all that, the table continues to be that common, everyday thing, wood. But, so soon as it steps forth as a commodity, it is changed into something transcendent. It not only stands with its feet on the ground, but, in relation to all other commodities, it stands on its head, and evolves out of its wooden brain grotesque ideas, far more wonderful than "table-turning" ever was.[70]

The simple product of human activity takes on a whole new significance, way beyond its natural properties.

Commodity fetishism

While Marx's analysis of commodity fetishism can help understand the kinds of developments Klein describes, it is important to stress the difference between his analysis and much popular commentary on so-called "consumer culture". Firstly, for Marx commodity fetishism had nothing to do with the particular features of the commodities themselves—it is not about some alluring or corrupting qualities that a Kindle has that a book doesn't have, or about music produced by an iPod rather than an orchestra. Often, commentary on consumerism suggests that there is something inherently wrong with the products that we are being encouraged to buy. For example, the American liberal Henry David Thoreau, still popular in radical circles today, argued that "it is preoccupation with possessions, more than anything else, that prevents us from living freely and nobly".

The idea here is that having *too much stuff* is in some way the root of the problem. For Marx, however, it was not the things themselves that were the problem but the social relationships in which we produce, own and exchange those things. There is nothing at all wrong with products that make human lives more bearable, or more fun, nor is there anything wrong with poor and desperate people wanting those products.

The second important difference in Marx's account is that it emphasises that these fetishes should not be understood as *merely* illusion. Anti-consumerism campaigns often emphasise people simply consuming less, abandoning their illusions and desires. This kind of attitude is what underlies projects like "Buy Nothing Day", in which people are encouraged to stop buying things they want or need. The idea here is that our attitude to commodities is an illusion which we should try to see through and abandon.

However, central to Marx's account is that fetishism is not just an illusion. Rather, the perception of

Alienation

commodities as possessing a life of their own is a reflection of capitalist production, a necessary outgrowth of it. In Volume 1 of *Capital*, Marx corrects the Italian economist Galiani by pointing out that when he said "value is a relation between persons" he ought to have added, "a relation concealed beneath a material shell".[71] In pointing to this "material shell", Marx was observing that these "illusions" are rooted in the real relations between people. He insists that the analysis of commodities undertaken by himself and other political economists "marks an epoch in the history of mankind's development, but by no means banishes the semblance of objectivity possessed by the social characteristics of labour".[72]

Overcoming this fetishism cannot, therefore, be a matter of merely pointing out that it exists (although this helps). It is necessary to transform the social relations themselves. The experience of commodities as having a life of their own, as controlling rather than controlled, is a reflection of a system where products *are* out of the control of the majority.

The analysis of commodity fetishism also forms an important part of Marx's criticism of mainstream economics and the political economy of his day. He argued that mainstream economics focuses only on the fetishised form of economic relationships. The kinds of concepts and categories that economics uses are merely the fetishised reflections of real social relationships. Marx argues that, "to what extent some economists are misled by the fetishism inherent in commodities... is shown...by the dull and tedious quarrel over the part played by nature in the formation of exchange-value".[73] A concept like "value" is based on a social relationship; you will not discover the value of a commodity through looking at it, no matter how closely you look: "So far no chemist has ever discovered exchange value either in a pearl or a diamond".[74] However, mainstream economics treats this as a property of the object itself, something to do with its physical nature rather than social relationships.

This also indicates the role that fetishism can have in maintaining the capitalist system. The economic laws which are particular to capitalism become seen as universal, unchangeable laws of human society. These laws, "which bear it stamped upon them in unmistakable letters that they belong to a state of society, in which the process of production has the mastery over man, instead of being controlled by him...appear to the bourgeois intellect to be as much a self-evident necessity imposed by nature as productive labour itself".[75] When the form that capitalism takes is seen as a fundamental feature of objects in the world, as in some way *natural*, then it becomes far harder to challenge it.

Fetishism also influences the way in which we relate to each other. Because we relate through commodities, we tend to relate to each other through the form these commodities take. Thus aspects of our social and personal life become commodified and take on a particular value form. The starkest example of this is probably the commodification of sexuality. The sex industry is vast. It is worth $57 billion a year in revenue, including $20 billion a year from adult videos and $11 billion a year from escort services.[76] This involves an undeniable aspect of our humanity, our sexuality, being packaged and sold back to us. Sex itself becomes a commodity. In turn, sexualised imagery, overwhelmingly of women, comes to dominate all sorts of aspects of culture. Sex is used to advertise a vast range of products, and women's bodies become symbols of anything from alcohol to valve caps. You only need to think about the prevalence of the Playboy bunny, emblazoned on jewellery, T-shirts and even pencil cases, to see the extent this reaches.

This cannot fail to affect those sexual relationships that are not directly commodified. Not all sex is bought and sold, but in a society where we relate to each other through commodities it begins to take on certain characteristics. As Sheila McGregor puts it, the sex industry "reinforces the gender division of women as sexual objects and men as buyers of the product. This division traps women in a denial of their own sexual needs and men in the belief that women are bodies to be ogled at or bought".[77] Sexuality itself becomes understood through the form of value and commodities.

Commodity fetishism thus forms an important bridge between Marx's economic analysis of capitalism and his radical criticism of it. The commodity form, which is crucial to understanding the economics of capitalism, also pervades every aspect of our social life under capitalism, and leaves no aspect of our personal relationship untouched.

Chapter 7

Alienation from others

Marx saw labour, because of its collective character, as being important in shaping the way people interact with one another. When this labour is alienated it comes to have widespread consequences for our social life and relationships with others. Marx writes:

> An immediate consequence of man's estrangement from the products of his labour, his life activity, his species-being, is the estrangement of man from man. When man confronts himself, he also confronts other men. What is true of man's relationship to his labour, to the product of his labour and to himself, is also true of his relationship to other men, and to the labour and the object of the labour of other men.[78]

Alienation does not merely involve a relationship between workers and their labour; it shapes and colours relationships between everyone in society. People become isolated and divided; they see their neighbours as hostile competitors rather than cooperative partners.

The terms of relationships between individuals become coloured by the logic of the capitalist system. Other human beings appear to us through economic categories. We relate to them not directly, but as customers, employers, managers or competitors. The Hungarian philosopher István Mészáros describes this as a process of "second-order mediations". Human labour plays a direct *mediating* role between human beings and the world; it is the way in which we relate to the external world.

Mészáros argues that "productive activity is *alienated activity* when it departs from its proper function of humanly mediating in the subject-object relationship between man and nature".[79] In other words, capitalism puts in place of this direct mediation a host of "second-order" mediations, instituted by capitalist relationships: "Man's productive activity cannot bring him fulfilment because the institutionalised second-order mediations interpose themselves between man and his activity, between man and nature, and between man and man".[80]

Most clearly, this division appears in the relationship between workers and bosses:

> If the product of labour does not belong to the worker, if it confronts him as an alien power, this is only possible because it belongs to a man other than the worker... If he relates to his own activity as unfree activity, then he relates to it as activity in the service, under the rule, coercion and yoke of another man.[81]

The division of society into classes with opposed interests means that people become artificially divided against one another. As long as one group's existence depends on the exploitation and domination of another, these kinds of divisions will remain.

Marx stressed the physical and practical consequences of this alienation. He describes vividly the barriers and divisions set up between working people and capitalists in his brief comments on housing:

> The cellar dwelling of the poor man is a hostile element...a dwelling which he cannot regard as his own hearth—where he might at last exclaim: "Here I am at home"—but where

instead he finds himself *in someone else's* house, in the house of a *stranger* who always watches him and throws him out if he does not pay his rent.[82]

This alienation is reinforced when workers see the contrast between the houses they are forced to live in and the wealth of the rich. The worker "is also aware of the contrast in quality between his dwelling and a human dwelling that stands in the *other* world, in the heaven of wealth".[83]

The alienation between workers and capitalists takes other concrete forms. Barbara Ehrenreich describes the way she was forced to take a variety of tests and questionnaires when applying for low paid jobs across America. These tests were, presumably, supposed to dispense with the necessity for bosses to ever physically interview their workers:

> At The Maids, a housecleaning service, I am given something called the "Accutrac personality test", which warns at the beginning that "Accutrac has multiple measures which detect attempts to distort or psych out the questionnaire". Naturally I "never" find it hard "to stop moods of self-pity", nor do I imagine that others are talking about me behind my back or believe that "management and employees will always be in conflict because they have different sets of goals". The real function of these tests, I decide, is to convey information not to the employer but to the potential employee, and the information being conveyed is always: You will have no secrets from us. We don't want your muscles and that portion of your brain that is directly connected to them, we want your innermost self.[84]

All of this serves to emphasise both the separation of capitalists and workers, and the domination of the one over the other.

However, there is not just alienation between classes; capitalism encourages division and alienation among classes. The system relies on capitalists being a "band of warring brothers", competing aggressively among themselves even while they stand united against the working class. Capitalism depends on some capitalists succeeding, and others failing, on mergers, hostile takeovers and price wars. These pit individual capitalists against one another in a ruthless fight to squeeze as much profit as possible out of the system.

This affects the working class too. Working people are encouraged to see themselves as individuals competing with their workmates, neighbours and even friends. This begins in the competition for jobs themselves, as people are encouraged, often quite humiliatingly, to compete for the attention of employers. Anyone who has had to search for a job will have heard the endless advice from employment agencies and governments urging you to find a way to "get ahead", to distinguish yourself from other workers and prove yourself better. Once in work, this process intensifies. People are encouraged to compete to be "employee of the month", or for performance-related bonuses. A union steward from the Vauxhall car plant at Ellesmere Port on Merseyside describes how being divided into teams with team leaders "puts pressure on the weakest member of the team to keep up with their team mates. It also creates a competitive atmosphere because people are vying for the position of team leader and more pay".[85]

This inevitably has consequences outside of work too, affecting our relationship with our neighbours, friends and family. The kind of commodity fetishism I described in the previous chapter contributes to competition among friends and neighbours for meaningless status items. Just as people look for some sort of confirmation in acquiring commodities, they are encouraged to measure themselves against others by exactly that standard.

This competition and division creates fertile ground for ideas that divide the working class. People are pitted against one another, are told to compete with their workmates and friends, and in this environment racism, sexism and homophobia can easily take root. It is only in a situation where workers are forced to compete with one another for a small number of jobs that nationalist slogans such as "British jobs for British workers" can become meaningful or attractive. These sorts of ideas rely on the alienation from others which is so widespread under capitalism.

This also means that people are less likely to challenge the system. Because people are alienated and divided from one another, they are less likely to look to collective solutions to their problems. Instead they will accept the logic of the system, and compete to get ahead within capitalism. So, for example, instead of engaging in collective action to try to improve their condition alongside their workmates, workers feel the pressure to get their head down and work hard, in the hope that they might get a pay rise or an extra bonus. People become more likely to believe that they can only get ahead at the expense of other people, that we are "all in it for ourselves". In the speech I quoted in the introduction, Jimmy Reid observes the "implicit acceptance of the concept and term 'the rat race'. The picture it conjures up is one where we are scurrying around scrambling for position, trampling on others, back-stabbing, all in pursuit of personal success".[86]

As the example of sexuality described in the previous chapter shows, no aspect of our personal relationships is free from the effects of alienation. Even family life, which can provide some respite from the outside world, is affected by it. This can also involve some of the most shocking examples of alienation. To pick just one, in March 2010 a baby in Korea starved to death while her parents spent 12 hours playing a game in an internet cafe which involved raising a virtual child.[87] This is at the most extreme end of mediated social relationships, where the immediate connection between parents and child has become subordinated to an entirely artificial relationship.

Marx also saw *politics* as a particular example of this social alienation. The idea that politics is something separate from ordinary people's lives, something done by other people, is a result of artificially separating certain aspects of our lives from others. Politics becomes transformed into something narrow and specific, done by a special class of people. This separation in turn encourages the idea that economic, social and political questions are in some way separate from one another. Think about the newspaper, which has separate sections for each of these fields, as if economic questions were not of political importance, and vice versa. It is common to hear people assert that certain things, even famine and war, are "not a political issue". Even the act of politics becomes an isolated experience—casting your vote once a year (at most) in a private box, isolated from collective debate. This also encourages disaffection from political questions, people saying that they "don't do politics", even while they daily fight against a bullying boss or complain about price rises.

An important aspect of this alienation is the state. For Marx the existence of a distinct state, set apart and separate from society, is the inevitable consequence of division into classes. This is reminiscent of the both Rousseau's and Hegel's analyses, which saw the state as the result of social alienation, transferring away certain functions of social life to particular bodies—the courts, police, judges, etc. However, for both these thinkers this alienation was an inevitable and largely positive thing, necessary for people to live fulfilling lives within society.

Rousseau and Hegel saw the state as a neutral force, while Marx argued that it was necessarily a feature of class divisions, and existed to cement the rule of one class over another:

At the same pace at which the progress of modern industry developed, widened, intensified the class antagonism between capital and labour, the state power assumed more and more the character of a national power of capital over labour, of a public force organised for social enslavement, of an engine of class despotism.[88]

The state claims to operate in the communal interest, ie in the interests of everyone. However, Marx argued that capitalism is defined by class divisions that cannot be reconciled. Thus, whenever the state intervenes to defend the "common interest", it in fact intervenes to defend the status quo, and thus the interests of the ruling class. What is in the interests of helping capitalism survive is very much not in the interests of the working class. Thus the state is a feature of capitalist production.

Just as commodity fetishism creates the impression that mere objects have an independent existence, so does social alienation create the impression of the state as an independent entity, beyond the people who make it up. And just like in commodity fetishism, this becomes more than mere illusion. The nation state comes to have significance way beyond the people who live in it, and it takes on a permanent life of its own. People's willingness to die "for their country" or even for "the flag" is testament to this. The community becomes embodied in objects and symbols, which are seen as somehow "more" than the community itself.

More broadly than the state, however, this social alienation also gives rise to the sense that much of human life is outside of our control. Despite our social and economic life being entirely the product of human activity, it is experienced as a disembodied, alien power. As Marx puts it, throughout history human beings have "become more and more enslaved under a power alien to them...a power which has become more and more enormous and, in the last instance, turns out to be the world market".[89] You only need to watch the TV news to see how this kind of thinking begins to take hold. Stock market movements are reported like changes in the weather, with stock going up and down in value as if the result of a natural process. In the 2010 election in Britain "the markets" were said to demand a quick resolution to the hung parliament, and even more sinisterly, said to have a preferred outcome.

This feature of alienation affects everyone, even those at the top of the system. As Marx put it, "the immanent laws of capitalist production confront the individual capitalist as a coercive force external to him".[90] They are slaves to the pressures of the market, and completely subject to its whims. However, capitalists experience alienation in a different way. Their wealth enables them to be cushioned from some of its worst effects, and in as much as the system is organised in their interests the effects of alienation are not so severe. Despite this, capitalists are incapable of finding fulfilment in their work, just as workers are. Often capitalists are merely passive exploiters who grow rich on the back of the work of others. When they do "work", it is generally at finding new and intricate ways of squeezing more profit from those workers. As Bertell Ollman puts it, "the capitalists' advantages over the proletariat are relative rather than absolute; they concern registering a higher score on a scale which itself must be condemned".[91]

Chapter 8

Alienation from self

Capitalism is not just bad for us socially, Marx argued, it is also bad for us individually. Marx wrote that the worker "does not confirm himself in his work, but denies himself, feels miserable and not happy, does not develop free mental and physical energy, but mortifies his flesh and ruins his mind".[92]

This aspect of Marx's critique was motivated largely by his analysis and experience of the proletariat in his own time. Here he observed the physical and psychological damage done to workers by factory conditions. The most significant feature was not the factory work itself, but the way it was organised so as to put the needs of production and profit before the needs of the worker. In Marx's economic works he details many of the diverse kinds of factory production, and how they affect the lives of the workers. To take just one example, he describes the change in printing workers brought about by the printing machine:

> In the English letter-press printing trade there existed formerly a system, corresponding to that in the old manu- factures and handicrafts, of advancing the apprentices from easy to more and more difficult work. They went through a course of teaching till they were finished printers. To be able to read and write was for every one of them a require- ment of their trade. All this was changed by the printing machine. It employs two sorts of labourers, one grown up, renters, the other, boys mostly from 11 to 17 years of age

whose sole business is either to spread the sheets of paper under the machine, or to take from it the printed sheets. They perform this weary task, in London especially, for 14, 15, and 16 hours at a stretch, during several days in the week, and frequently for 36 hours, with only two hours' rest for meals and sleep. A great part of them cannot read, and they are, as a rule, utter savages and very extraordinary creatures.

Many of these new processes involved damage to health and fitness, but actually made it easier for workers to perform their work. One example of this is the permanent changes to the shape of workers' bones which resulted from the use of certain machinery. Features that would be a problem for an artisan, who had to do many different jobs in a working day, were in fact beneficial when only one action was performed repetitively for eight to ten hours a day. In this way workers are converted "into a living appendage of the machine", and their own health and life is subordinated to the needs of production. Their work shapes and defines their very identity, getting under their skin—in some cases literally. In St Helens, a town in the Northwest of England dominated by glass production, it used to be remarked that, "You can recognise a fibreglass worker by the fact he's always scratching".[93]

It is worth emphasising that these sorts of health problems related to working conditions have hardly gone away. The suicides in 2010 at the Foxconn factory, which manufactures parts for the iPad, brought to attention the prevalence of mass factory conditions. Workers report that "their hands continue to twitch at night, or that when they are walking down the street they cannot help but mimic the motion".[94] In response to the suicides Foxconn put up a net around the factory to catch people jumping. A study of call centres found that the pressures and processes of work have severe implications for employee well-being: "Workers were subject to feelings of exhaustion and not being able to 'switch off' after work and, more seriously, feelings of stress and, occasionally, even adverse health consequences".[95]

A worker reports on his first week working at a British car plant:

> Everyone is chatting away when they can, and then someone asks about Tom, who has been off for a few weeks with back pain from an injury he got when lifting a hood onto a jig when the automatic feeder broke down. It's like lifting the lid on a pressure cooker. Some can't stop talking about the various physical injuries. Things they "just have to carry on with". But it's not only the physical pain, which someone points out to me later most people have to put up with "as long as you can cope", but also the mental stress of not making mistakes, and it's worse too with the mental isolation.[96]

Even in the absence of mass factory conditions, there remains a big difference between workplaces designed for the needs of profit and of regulating the workforce and the kind of workplaces that are best for our health. A study of clerical and office workplaces in Glasgow argued, "Our respondents' comments confirm that a crucial ingredient of a healthy and agreeable working environment is the degree to which the worker can exercise control over it".[97] However, the way these buildings are designed tends to be the exact opposite of this. What is valued is cost reduction and workforce control: "Current practice is an overwhelmingly technology-centred, top-down operation in which the environmental system is installed and then people are expected to adjust".[98]

More broadly, Marx was concerned with the impact of social relationships on our physical and mental health. It was not just the kind of work which was important, but the relationships of power and control within them. Class, therefore,

Alienation

was of vital importance. The lack of control over their working and private lives experienced by members of the working class played a crucial role in explaining their ill-health.

Marx's arguments are consistent with a number of recent findings in studies of health and illness. Many studies have shown a close connection between social status and health problems. In general, the poorer you are, the less you have in society, the greater your risk of developing health problems. Class and class divisions shape people's early lives, their friendships, social relationships, leisure time and working conditions. All of these have a profound effect on their long-term health.

A key indicator of this is social inequality. Richard Wilkinson and Kate Pickett's popular book *The Spirit Level* offers important insights into how much inequality can affect societies. The greater the gap between the richest and the poorest in society the worse off people are likely to be. Significantly this is not merely a matter of material deprivation. It is not simply a matter of the poor being very poor, and suffering as a result. Rather it is a direct feature of the inequality within society; of the rich being very, very, very rich. Even in countries where the poor are comparatively better off than in other countries, the existence of hierarchies and inequalities contributes directly to poor physical and mental health. In fact, recent studies have suggested that a whole range of things are directly affected by inequality—teenage pregnancy, crime, mental health, life expectancy and so on.

The same physical health risks impact differently depending on your position within a society. A study of civil servants found a close connection between their rank, the amount of control they have over their work, and their health: "An administrator who smokes 20 cigarettes a day has a lower risk of dying from lung cancer than does a lower grade civil

Alienation from self   65 servant who smokes the same amount".[99] The conclusion was that "having control at work was the most successful single factor explaining threefold differences in death rates between senior and junior civil servants working in the same government offices in Britain".[100] A similar report concludes that "giving employees more variety in tasks and a stronger say in decisions about work may decrease the risk of coronary heart disease".[101]

All of this suggests that it is not just inequality in the distribution of wealth or social status alone that causes these problems, but alienation. The roots of these problems are to be found in the way in which our social and working lives are organised, and that is first and foremost defined by a lack of control. It is not just the gap between the richest and the poorest but the division between bosses and workers that affects our health and well-being. Inequality is likely to be an indicator of class position and alienation—those with least control over their work are also likely to be the least paid and vice versa—but it is not the root cause.

Because we lack the opportunity to express ourselves through fulfilling, creative work, we look for other ways of exerting control over our lives. This means that our personal lives come to be seen as the sole means of expressing our individuality. At work we are faceless, powerless and interchangeable; at home we try to express our individuality through the food we eat, the clothes we wear, the music we listen to, the cars we drive and the relationships we form.

For most people, though, this is fairly limited. They can't afford much more than mass-produced identical things, and the demands of work constantly impact on this individuality. This, in part, explains the obsession with celebrity culture which is so widespread under modern capitalism. These are people whose individuality is taken seriously, and generally have the means to achieve it. As Colin Sparks puts it:

Alienation

The realm of celebrity is the realm of legitimised personality. One of the key characteristics of celebrities is that their private lives and doings are taken to be interesting and treated as public property. This is often denounced as an intolerable intrusion, but in fact it is the highest reward that can be bestowed under capitalism. Unlike the mass of the population, the celebrity is someone whose individuality is taken seriously.[102]

The obsession with celebrity culture comes from a desire to have our individuality taken seriously in a way that capitalism consistently denies to the immense majority. Of course, this offers no real challenge to the alienation which gives rise to it. It might give people temporary respite, but it does not overcome their alienation.

Often people look to reassert control over their lives in even more dramatic ways. For example, according to a 2006 study, "An estimated 1.2 million young people [in Japan have] retreated from all contact with the outside world into the confines of their own rooms—modern hermits or *hikikomori*".[103] These young people are quite literally alienated, cutting themselves off from the world and others completely.

A feeling of not having control also plays a notable role in many eating disorders, in particular anorexia nervosa. Studies of anorexia patients suggest that control plays a significant part in their attitudes towards the disorder. The following quotations all come from a 2006 study of ten female anorexia patients aged between 13 and 21 and their parents.[104] The disorder is seen as a means of asserting control: "If I was fat then I would be unattractive and a complete failure, and completely not in control of what I do and what I ate"; "She's got control over it, the only thing she can control is her body." Control also figures in attitudes towards treatment:

As soon as I was in a place where I was in control and choice and everything then I just wanted to be healthy and the figures weren't so relevant, it was how I felt and stuff. I really think that if I'd stayed in a place that was really rigid I'd have lost it all again... But coming to a place where it's all my choice and in my control then I could really work out what I wanted and it works so much better for me that way.

The report noted that some suggested the disorder would "help them feel safe and in control especially in difficult times". In a world in which so much is outside of the control of most people, people look to assert control in any way they can, often with tragic consequences.

Mental health problems under capitalism are rife. Just taking Britain as an example, it is estimated that one in six of the adult population suffer from depression or chronic anxiety disorder (around six million people), meaning that one in three families are directly affected by it. Forty percent of disability is due to mental, rather than physical, illness. One report concluded that "crippling depression and chronic anxiety are the biggest causes of misery in Britain today".[105]

Yet despite widespread agreement on the depth of the problem of mental health, there is a remarkable tendency to ignore the wider social context, to treat these as problems for individuals rather than society as a whole, and to look to solutions in individual therapy or medication. The same report that identified the prevalence of depression in Britain also restricted its proposed solutions to making Cognitive Behavioural Therapy more available to ordinary people. The question was not posed as "How can we organise society to stop this happening?" but "How can we get more people medication and therapy?" This often combined the well-meaning with the sinister—for example, therapy in job centres, with half a mind on helping people, but the other half on getting them back to work as quickly as possible.

In other words, as well as contributing to worsening mental health, alienation provides a barrier to overcoming it. Firstly, proposed solutions are driven by the need to get people back to work, and to make profit. Thus the real problems are often not addressed at all. Secondly, alienation contributes to a failure to address these problems as rooted in social relationships. Just like the economist who examines a commodity to find its value, ignoring that the value is socially constituted, so medical professionals tend to examine people as individuals, looking for internal causes of their problems, and ignoring the clearly social causes.

More broadly, alienation shapes even what we define as mental health problems. In the report cited above, the overwhelming focus was on conditions that interfere with people's working lives, making them less productive individuals in the labour process. Much of it is pitched in terms of the economic damage that depression does to the UK economy. This is framed entirely in terms of the needs of capitalism, not the needs of the individual. As Peter Sedgwick argues, definitions of illness and fitness depend on the goals society sets.[106] In a society organised on the basis of wage-labour, anything which interferes with this is seen as an illness to be managed or cured. A society organised according to different priorities could offer a different understanding of illness, and also offer alternative ways of helping those who suffer.

Chapter 9

Alienation from nature

One aspect of alienation that is hugely relevant to the modern world is alienation from nature. There is widespread consensus about the role of human activity in bringing about changes in the climate which could be disastrous. Increase in global temperatures due to greenhouse gas emissions threatens destruction on an unprecedented scale. For example:

> A temperature rise of 1.5 degrees will expose an extra 400 million people to water stress and a further 5 million to hunger. Coral reefs will become extinct in the Indian Ocean. 18 percent of the world's flora and fauna will die out.[107]

It is not just in climate change where human activity is impacting on the natural world. Waste, pollution and environmental destruction are rife.

Despite this overwhelming consensus, and the knowledge of how it could be stopped, very little is being done about this. Nowhere was this clearer than on the Isle of Wight in the summer of 2009, where Britain's only wind turbine manufacturer, owned by a company called Vestas, closed. The then energy secretary Ed Miliband, despite his professed commitment to combating climate change, allowed it to close. Ultimately market forces were more important than any commitment to renewable energy. Thankfully workers at Vestas had other ideas, and organised an occupation which lasted many months.

There is a myth that Marx and Engels, and therefore Marxists, have nothing to say about, or even can be hostile to, environmentalism. Certainly some who have called themselves Marxists have a bad track record in this regard. In particular, the view of Marx as someone with a disregard for the environment and nature was given credence by the environmental problems associated with the rapid industrialisation of the Stalinist states. However, this ignores the rich contribution made by Marx, Engels and later Marxists to environmental questions. Recent research, notably by Marxist ecologists such as John Bellamy Foster, has shown how Marx's insights about alienation from nature are of great importance to understanding the social processes that have brought us to the brink of environmental catastrophe, and seem to prevent us from pulling back.

Marx and Engels were writing at a time when there was very little knowledge of the impact of human activity on the environment, and even less of a sense of the science involved. However, during the Enlightenment various thinkers had begun to develop an analysis which focused on the connection between human society and apparently "natural" phenomena. One example was the reaction to an earthquake in Lisbon in 1755. This disaster had a strong influence on philosophers and social theorists. The French philosopher Voltaire used it to argue against the idea that we lived in the best of all possible worlds, pointing out the heartlessness of the natural world. Rousseau, on the other hand, argued that the disaster was not solely a natural one, but a social one caused by the building of fragile, tall buildings in dangerous areas. It was a result of unnatural ways of living that failed to respect environmental surroundings.

In the *Economic and Philosophical Manuscripts* Marx made a number of very general remarks about the damage that capitalism does to the relationship between humans and nature. He writes that in being alienated from the product of their labour the worker "at the same time" relates "to the sensuous external world, to the objects of nature, as an alien world inimically opposed to him". This is because:

> Man *lives* on nature...with which he must remain in continuous interchange if he is not to die. That man's physical and spiritual life is linked to nature means simply that nature is linked to itself, for man is a part of nature.[108]

Thus our alienation from the products and process of labour means that we also become alienated from the natural world in which we live and work. Just as work confronts us as alien and out of control, so does the natural world.

Marx and Engels developed these early ideas as part of an analysis of the role of land in economics. They were concerned with addressing the popular ideas of Malthus—versions of which still form part of common sense today. According to Malthus, famine was periodically inevitable because human population necessarily grew faster than its capacity to produce food. Thus human population would reach points of crisis where there was simply not enough food to feed everyone. Marx saw Malthus's ideas as giving "brutal expression to the brutal viewpoint of capital". Malthus's error was to assume a fixed limit to the growth of food production which was independent of the different ways in which that production was organised. He, with no good reason, "asserted the fact of overpopulation in all forms of society".

But overpopulation was a relative thing, and food production was limited far more by external constraints than by any "natural" laws of its production. The limits of these sorts of ideas became increasingly clear during the rapid growth in use and production of fertilisers in the middle of the 19th century. Agricultural production was able to grow rapidly, well beyond what was previously thought possible. However, this agricultural revolution brought with it new problems. It was driven by the needs of capitalist expansion, in particular the needs of feeding the vast new populations of workers in the cities. Capitalism had created the proletariat, and concentrated them in particular places of work, with no land or means to feed themselves. Now they needed to be fed.

Foremost among these new problems was that of soil erosion. It was increasingly clear that industrialisation was eroding soil by extracting nutrients from it which were never replaced, but rather dumped as waste in the cities. The growth of mass cities, and the kinds of production and transport that this involved, was leading to a situation where the soil was not fertile enough to produce the food required by demand. In *Capital* Marx wrote:

> Capitalist production collects the population together in great centres, and causes the urban population to achieve an ever-growing preponderance. This has two results. On the one hand it concentrates the historical motive force of society; on the other hand, it disturbs the metabolic interaction between man and the earth, ie it prevents the return to the soil of its constituent elements consumed by man in the form of food and clothing; hence it hinders the operation of the eternal natural condition for the lasting fertility of the soil... All progress in capitalist agriculture is a progress in the art, not only of robbing the worker, but of robbing the soil.[109]

Marx identifies here a breakdown in the reciprocal relationship between nature and human beings due to concentrations of population. Engels observed that "in London alone a greater quantity of manure than is produced by the whole kingdom of Saxony is poured away every day into the sea with an expenditure of enormous sums".[110] It was therefore necessary to re-establish an "intimate connection between industrial and agricultural production" together with "as uniform a distribution as possible of the population over the whole country".[111]

Central to this account was the concept of metabolism (in German *Stoffwechsel*, literally "material exchange"). Marx's later writings increasingly employ the concept of metabolism to describe the relationship between human beings and nature. He describes labour as "a process between man and nature, a process by which man, through his own actions, mediates, regulates and controls the metabolism between himself and nature".[112] In the example of soil erosion there is a literal failure of "material exchange", where nutrients drawn from the soil in the process of growing crops are not adequately replaced. This breakdown of natural processes was the result of the demands of capitalism for a workforce concentrated in cities.

This kind of breakdown is a result of the loss of control of the labour process. If labour plays a central role in mediating between human beings and nature, then loss of control of that mediating relationship has disastrous consequences. The metabolism between human beings and nature has broken down, become irregular and uneven. John Bellamy Foster has developed an account of alienation from nature based on the notion of a "metabolic rift". As Foster notes, "the German word *Stoffwechsel* directly sets out in its elements the notion of 'material exchange' that underlies the notion of structured processes of biological growth and decay captured in the term metabolism". Foster argues, "The concept of metabolism provided Marx with a concrete way of expressing the notion of the alienation of nature...that was central to his critique from his earliest writings on".[113] It gives scientific flesh to the arguments about the relationship between man and nature offered in the *Economic and Philosophical Manuscripts*. This notion of a metabolism between man and nature is especially relevant today. The failure to replace nutrients extracted from the soil (a problem which has not been resolved) parallels a failure to extract carbon dioxide emitted into the atmosphere.

It is important to note that Marx's account differs from accounts of alienation from nature, such as Rousseau's, which hark back to some sort of ideal natural state. For Marx it is not necessary that we return to a pre-modern condition of living which no longer exists. To be alienated from nature is not to be separated from a Garden of Eden to which we must return. Rather, alienation from nature, and the notion of metabolic rift, describe the lack of control over our relationship with nature which capitalism demands and encourages.

This is clear in some of Engels's writings on the relationship between town and country:

> Abolition of the antithesis between town and country is not merely possible. It has become a direct necessity of industrial production itself, just as it has become a necessity of agricultural production and, besides, of public health. The present poisoning of the air, water and land can be put an end to only by the fusion of town and country; and only such fusion will change the situation of the masses now languishing in the towns, and enable their excrement to be used for the production of plants instead of for the production of disease.[114]

This is not the idea of returning to a lost country life, but of abolishing the distinction between town and country. Furthermore, it is not motivated by some sort of mystical concern for nature, but the immediate needs of human health, and of a form of production better suited to meet human needs.

This also means that Marx would propose very different solutions from those fashionable among many environmentalists. These often focus on changing individual behaviour, on everyone reducing their "carbon footprint" on an individual level. Many even argue that the same market forces which have created this state of affairs could be invoked to solve it. One of the most popular solutions proposed to climate change is "carbon trading", whereby companies can continue to pollute on one side of the world in exchange for investing in renewable energy or planting trees on the other side. This could not be a clearer example of the consequences of commodity fetishism, where even CO_2 molecules are understood as commodities which can be traded off against one another. This creates yet more intricate ways for capitalists to line their pockets, but does little to solve the problem.

For Marx, alienation from nature, like all alienation, could only be overcome collectively, through the total reorganisation of society. This requires exerting conscious, collective control over this relationship, in which people "govern the human metabolism with nature in a rational way bringing it under their own collective control instead of being dominated by it as a blind power".[115] It involves an awareness of the delicate metabolism between humans and nature, and the ways in which this must be regulated and controlled on an individual and collective level. This does not involve any one particular model of organising human life, but it certainly rules out the one we currently have.

For Marx and Engels, alienation from nature was not the most urgent concern. However, its significance for the current generation cannot be ignored. Alienation from nature is fast becoming the most dangerous form of alienation of all for the human species.

Chapter 10

Has work changed?

The main driving force behind Marx's description was the model of large-scale factory production, in which workers became appendages to heavy machinery, necessary for the machine's operation, but also subject to its rhythms and demands. This system is alive and well for many people today. The Foxconn factory alone employs 300-400,000 workers, who live on site and work 70-hour weeks. It takes 30 minutes to drive around the factory from the west gate to the south gate. For millions around the world this kind of work is normal. The fact that the Foxconn factory produced the must-have gadget of 2011—the iPad—only reinforces how connected this kind of production is to the developed world.

However, in some forms and in some places, work has changed from what Marx described. Marx acknowledged the way capitalism rapidly revolutionises society, making all that is solid melt into air. Capitalism has thrown up new forms of work, particularly in the developed world, that Marx does not discuss. Does this mean that Marx's ideas do not apply today? According to many commentators, both defenders and critics of capitalism, Marx's ideas about work are outdated, and cannot be applied to the modern world.

Much is made of the fact that employment in manufacturing has shrunk significantly in Europe and the US in recent decades, while the service and financial sectors have grown. So, for example, since 1978 the percentage of the UK workforce in manufacturing has declined from 28.5 percent to just

10 percent.[116] In the same period there have been significant increases in the proportion of workers in the service sector, including a doubling of those in finance and business services, and 28.1 percent of workers work in public administration, education or health.[117] These jobs are often seen as offering more freedom for the individual worker. They are not as repetitive or degrading as the kind of factory work that Marx observed, and don't involve the same sorts of health risks.

There has also been a big change in the way managers talk about work, even in the "older" types of work. Workers are now familiar with their bosses talking nonsense about leadership and "employee autonomy". However, this rhetoric should not be taken at face value. Alienated social relationships and work practices, as Marx would have understood them, are alive and well today.

For Marx alienation was rooted in the social relationships that make up capitalism—the division of society into a class which owns the means of production and a class which has to sell its labour, and the transformation of labour into a commodity. The particular type of labour, and the particular type of workplace, is not the most important factor. Heavy machinery is not the main source of alienation. Marx certainly was concerned with the way in which heavy machinery dominated working life; however, he was more concerned with the social relationships and conditions of work that the new machinery created. The development of industry required the double freedom of the working class alongside relationships of strict command on the factory floor. These conditions can and do continue even when heavy machinery is absent. You don't literally need a conveyor belt to feel like you work on a production line. The key question is not the type of work done, but the relationships of command and control that it involves.

One of the most prominent arguments that Marx's analysis no longer applies in full comes from the work of Michael

Hardt and Toni Negri. Hardt and Negri are not apologists for capitalism. In fact they are fierce critics, who have been active and influential in the anti-capitalist movement. Negri in particular has a long history of radical activity in Italy. However, they argue that new forms of work have changed things in important ways. They claim that there has been a fundamental economic transformation to a "paradigm in which providing services and manipulating information are at the heart of economic production".[118] They argue that "the passage toward an informational economy necessarily involves a change in the quality and nature of labour".[119] This transformation has meant that a new form of labour is now dominant, what they call "immaterial labour", involving the production or manipulation of symbols, texts, emotions or feelings.

While Hardt and Negri do not think this work is necessarily better, they do think it opens new possibilities for the workers. One of the reasons for this is that all that is required for this kind of work, apparently, is our own brains: "Brains and bodies still need others to produce value, but the others they need are not necessarily provided by capital and its capacities to orchestrate production".[120] This means, effectively, that workers are no longer free in the double sense Marx describes. Workers no longer *have to* sell their labour power to a capitalist to survive. Negri makes this point quite explicitly in an interview in the *New Statesman*: "In the past, labour depended on capital to provide the factory and all the tools of production. Today, we have all the tools we need to work in our heads".[121]

While Hardt and Negri make these claims from a radical perspective, they are not so different from the kinds of claims put forward by management and theorists of very different political backgrounds. And these arguments can be absurdly exaggerated. For example, it is simply wrong to suggest, as the interview quoted above does, that these "new" kinds of work need only what we have in our head. Can a group of nurses group together to work without a hospital? Can call centre workers do their job without a call centre? Can cabin crew serve drinks without an aircraft? It is entirely unclear why these workers using their own brains is any different from a coal miner who owns his own hands or a truck driver who uses her own feet. They still need a workplace, equipment, etc, and these are all owned by capitalists.

Leaving aside Negri's more exaggerated claims about the nature of this work, Hardt and Negri are also wrong to argue that "immaterial labour" is now dominant over other forms of labour. Work and workers may look different from in Marx's day, but it is important to look past those superficial differences to see just how similar things are. Even in Marx's day, there were substantial service and financial sectors, but Marx understood them as serving the needs of manufacturing, not the other way round. This is true today. Just because, in the developed world at least, the so-called informational economy employs the greatest number of people, this does not mean it is the "dominant" part of the economy. Rather, it is important to remember that the manufacturing sector of the economy is still of great importance, and that the service and information sectors in general exist *because of* it.

Vodafone's workers in the UK may all be office, shop or call centre workers, but they exist to sell phones, which are manufactured, and the use of a network, which though "wireless" requires substantial transmitting equipment. Even if the designers, distributors, promoters and customer service providers of the iPhone are better paid and more numerous than its manufacturers, it doesn't make them any more integral to the process. It is notable that Apple overtook Microsoft recently as the largest technology company based not on software but on electronic gadgets, actual products that can be held in people's hands.

Despite the promises of both management and some on the left, the evidence for any real changes in the nature of work is very limited. There is a very strong tendency to make sweeping generalisations about new kinds of work. A member of British Airways cabin crew and a worker in a Department of Work and Pensions call centre may both be very different from a production line worker at Jaguar Land Rover, but they are also very different from each other. Instead of making theoretical abstractions from the apparent common features of these jobs, it seems more useful to consider the concrete workplace relations they involve.

Yet arguments for the new kind of work have tended to be remarkably weak when it comes to providing analysis of the actual workplace. As one study argued, these debates tend to "assume, rather than empirically examine, changing work practices and through a leap of faith move on to discuss the enhanced class position of knowledge workers and the managerial challenge they pose".[122] Arguments such as Hardt and Negri's, which assert that these forms of work *can* or *will* bring with them a new kind of worker, tend to leap over demonstrating that they *have* or *are*:

> In fact, there is much evidence to the contrary. Rather than assuming and asserting that with the emergence of knowledge workers a revolution has occurred, the key question now seems to be: why hasn't the revolution happened?[123]

One reason to think work has changed is that some jobs appear to be much more complex compared with the sort of production line work that Marx described. Marx described work being divided up into ever smaller, simple tasks, which would necessarily stunt workers' creativity. However, in some cases this has not happened. It might be thought that as jobs become more complicated, they necessarily need more employee control, which can alleviate the worst aspects of alienation.

However, a comparison of survey results from 1986 and 2001 looking at skill levels in Britain suggests that this is not the case, and in fact precisely the opposite trend appears. While the comparison suggests small but steady increases in the complexity and skill levels of jobs in Britain, there was no corresponding increase in the amount of "task discretion"[124]—ie of control workers can exercise over their jobs. In fact, "there has been a marked decline in task discretion".[125] The proportion of employees reporting "a great deal" of choice over the way they do their job declined from 51.8 percent in 1986 to 38.68 percent in 2001, while those reporting a great deal of influence over how hard to work declined from 70.78 percent in 1992 to 50.68 percent in 2001.[126]

What this suggests is that whatever changes the new industries are bringing, they do not involve an increase in control over work. In a study of three clerical workplaces in Glasgow, two public sector and one private, in the late 1990s, the conclusion was that "the configuration of work, atmosphere and level of surveillance was more akin to a light manufacturing assembly plant than to conventional images of office work".[127]

The study argues that "there is little to show from our case studies and interviews with operatives that the new forms of working prevalent in call centres were being matched by new styles or approaches to management", and concludes that "despite the promise of 'new' work improving employees' working lives and expanding opportunities for all, we found the reality to be very different".[128]

Even in manufacturing there has been in a shift in the way management talk about their industry. For example, Hardt and Negri make a great deal of the transition in how car factories are organised from Fordism to Toyotism. While Fordism emphasised simplified routine tasks, Toyotism emphasised team working and employee freedom. But once again the reality of these new forms of management doesn't live up to the promises. A study of Japanese firms in South Wales casts

Alienation

significant doubt on the how different these new methods really are. The "Japanese model" supposedly involves team working, which "mobilises a sense of 'ownership', autonomy and business orientation". It is supposed to "provide some space for direct production workers to participate in job design".[129]

Yet in practice this simply doesn't happen. Far from being given creative freedom, "without exception production operators were employed on a variety of low-skill, monotonous and repetitive tasks".[130] When questioned about "ownership" a trade union steward at Matsushita Electric responded:

> Ownership of work? You've got to challenge this terminology strongly. What's it supposed to mean? You have only got the bloody unit in front of you for two seconds. So how are you supposed to own it?[131]

In fact, the only particularly distinctive feature of the Japanese model that the study identifies is the extreme degree of control asserted over employees' working time, in particular the meticulous working to bells and sirens. "Japanese management practice is conspicuous for its generally meticulous approach to labour regulation, which in turn, is aimed at securing enhanced leverage over effort and worker compliance to boot".[132]

Another important difference between Marx's world and our own is the vast expansion of the state sector. Far more people are employed in public services than were in the 19th century. The state is a huge employer, and it cannot be separated off from the wider capitalist economy. Conservative rhetoric claims that the state is a drain on the economy. They claim that it doesn't produce any value and stifles private industry, and this suits their purposes when they want to cut back on benefits and jobs. But the state plays an essential role in capitalism. For Marx, labour power is a commodity, and the most important commodity for the functioning of capitalism. The state sector has to be understood as playing a role in the *reproduction* of this labour power, ie creating and maintaining a healthy and able workforce. Health, welfare and education are all necessary to create working people who are adequately skilled and fit for the labour process.

This means that the 28.1 percent of people in public services or administration should not be seen as simply outside of the system of production. Rather, they are an integral part of reproducing the workforce. Furthermore, working in these jobs is not some sort of paradise of employee autonomy when compared to the private sector. Public sector workers are subject to a great deal of bureaucratic pressure to meet targets and provide a quantifiable service. For example, Michael Lavalette and Iain Ferguson describe the increasingly managerial and bureaucratic work environment within social work and its extremely negative effects: "The consequence is that social workers find they have less freedom and control over their contact and work with clients; they are subject to speed-up, bureaucratic control and regulation; their work activities increasingly confront them and their clients as a set of 'alien' practices".[133]

There is a conflict between the role of social workers as socially conscious carers, interested in the care of their clients, and their role as reproducers of labour power, under pressure to get people back into work as quickly as possible. It is important to stress the connection between this and Marx's discussion of abstract labour. The work of public sector workers is measured, restricted and quantified. Heaps of paperwork, targets, tests and assessments are piled up in front of all public sector workers. As the examples from higher education in Chapter 4 suggest, the aim of this is to quantify both the labour they *do* and the labour they *reproduce*— ie how much they enable *others* to work. This drive towards bureaucratisation, and attempts to quantify work performed, pull sharply away from any sense of fulfilment in such work.

What is striking in each case here is the gap between the reality of people's working lives and the rhetoric of a radical new kind of work. In both the study of the call centres and the Japanese manufacturing firms the reality was very different from the rhetoric *both* of management and of a number of social theorists. As Kevin Doogan has noted, this gap between the assumptions about how work has changed and its reality suggests that there is often a highly politicised dimension to these debates.[134] Often those who exaggerate the way in which work has changed have a hidden (though often not very well hidden) political agenda. The exaggerated rhetoric of a new age of work hides just how much remains stubbornly the same as the world Marx described.

This gap between reality and rhetoric can itself contribute to alienation. One feature of recent years has been an increase in the number of workers who are "over-qualified" for their jobs—in the study of call centres over a quarter of workers had degree-level or higher qualifications. When the expectation of a new form of fulfilling, creative, qualified work is met with a mundane, routinised and unfulfilling reality it can contribute to a sense of alienation and powerlessness. Martin Smith describes his first day as a civil servant in the Passport Office:

> I made the terrible mistake of thinking I was going up in the world. I arrived at work wearing my best suit... I got the shock of my life: everyone else was wearing jeans. I ended up being assigned to a huge office, where half the people opened letters all day and the other stuffed envelopes... I was part of a clerical production line.[135]

Exaggerated claims of the end of alienation can in this way actually serve to exacerbate alienation. Far from ushering in a new era of unalienated work, the new forms of work and management bring with them new dimensions of alienation, and do little to abolish the old ones.

Has work changed?

Chapter 11

Species-being and controversies of interpretation

In this chapter I want to raise and comment on a few of the disagreements around interpreting Marx's theory of alienation. Several controversies have developed in interpreting Marx's work, particularly on the question of the extent to which his ideas changed over his lifetime.

Marx wrote over a period of 35 years, during which he witnessed uprisings, revolutions and the growth of a mass workers' movement. This period also coincided with great scientific and technological developments, as well as shifts in philosophy and social theory. In this context it would be bizarre if Marx's ideas did not change in some ways. However, there is disagreement about how much his ideas changed. Broadly, there are those who see some sort of "essential unity" in Marx's work, and those who believe his work has to be divided into different periods where he is dealing with different subjects and problems.

According to those who suggest an essential unity, Marx spent his life developing the concepts that came about in his early criticism of Hegel. While some of his terminology changed, the essential ideas remained the same. So, for example, Mészáros argues that "the concept of alienation, as grasped by Marx in 1844...is a vitally important pillar of the Marxian system as a whole".[136] On the other hand, others argue that at certain points Marx's emphasis shifts. Most commonly, this involves some sort of division between the "young Marx" and the "mature Marx". The young Marx is seen as a radical Hegelian, still concerned fundamentally with Hegel's problems—*philosophical* problems. The mature Marx shifts to questions of economics and social science. A very influential advocate of this was the French Marxist Louis Althusser, who argued that there was a radical shift in Marx's focus after the mid-1840s.

This is important for considerations of alienation. Alienation is a concept which occurs most explicitly in Marx's early work, and is most detailed in his *Economic and Philosophical Manuscripts* of 1844. The word alienation tends to fade out of Marx's later works. It is certainly mentioned less obviously in his more mature economic works, and in his masterpiece, *Capital*. Similarly, Marx tends to move away from a focus on philosophical questions, towards what he describes as a scientific approach. Philosophy increasingly appears as something to be rejected. This has led commentators to argue that the kind of philosophical questions raised by alienation are not relevant to the later Marx, and should be rejected.

But this is far from evident. There is no explicit evidence that Marx abandoned his ideas on alienation. Furthermore, while alienation does not occur in *Capital*, it is frequently mentioned in the *Grundrisse*, a collection of economic manuscripts written before *Capital* which deal with many of the same themes. For every piece of text which might support this view, there is something to suggest the opposite. Furthermore, concepts such as metabolism, mediation and commodity fetishism, which I have suggested are closely connected to a theory of alienation, actually appear *more* in the later Marx. The concept of commodity fetishism is central to the opening chapters of *Capital*. Much of this interpretation rests on whether you see commodity fetishism as a *development* of the notion of alienation from product or a *replacement* for it. As Chapter 6 suggests, I would argue that it is a development.

A similar controversy can arise in Marx's attitude towards work. In the way I have presented it, Marx sees labour as the way in which people can find fulfilment in the world. Under capitalism, work is anything but fulfilling, but under different conditions the way we labour could become genuinely meaningful. On this kind of vision, work, as genuinely fulfilling work, is something to be encouraged, and increased. However, elsewhere, particularly in his later writings, Marx tends to talk about minimising work. He argues that the great productive possibilities of capitalism mean that work can be vastly reduced, leaving people more time for recreational activity and so on.

There might appear to be a contradiction between Marx on the one hand emphasising the importance of work for human beings and on the other hand endorsing the reduction of the working day to a minimum. If work can be made fulfilling, why should it be minimised? However, there isn't necessarily a contradiction. It is entirely possible both to endorse the minimising of necessary labour, while continuing to encourage far more work beyond what is necessary. Marx clearly believed that minimising the amount of necessary work would not lead to a reduction in the amount of labour people performed. Rather, it would create more space for that labour to be creative, free and fulfilling. Furthermore, Marx also believed that *all* work, even that necessary to meet immediate human need, could be made far more fulfilling, and transformed from a burden to a creative activity.

Some people argue that whether or not Marx actively rejected a theory of alienation, he should have done. This is because the theory of alienation seems to rest on a theory of human nature. As I described above, in rejecting Feuerbach's arguments Marx shifted his focus away from a human nature inherent in any individual, and onto social relations, particularly *productive* relationships. However, at least in the way

I have presented it, there remains an idea of species-being whereby certain ways of organising production allow for more self-realisation than others. While this does not necessarily specify any *particular* model of how humans should organise society, of "the good life", it clearly identifies some ways of organising social life which are necessarily worse.

However, if Marx was being consistent, some argue, he would have rejected even this idea. This is because they see any idea of a human nature, even one as broad as that implied by the theory of alienation, as implausible—suggesting an idealised vision of human society which has no grounding in reality. For one thing, they argue, we cannot *know* how human beings might be different if they organised work in different ways. For another, this seems to go against Marx's vision of human nature as being *changeable*. In *Capital* Marx seems to be concerned with the capitalist system as an autonomous process. In these passages it seems as if humans are completely changeable, with no nature apart from that granted to them by their place in a structure.

The strongest argument against these ideas is the strength of Marx's theory of alienation itself. In the chapters above I have tried to argue that alienation is a concept that can genuinely help to understand many of the problems faced by human beings. A range of social and psychological experiences can be seen as having their roots in certain ways of organising production. Capitalism as a system breeds these ills, which cannot be reduced to mere questions of absolute poverty or material wealth. The theory of alienation offers a way of understanding how these things are connected, and how they might be different. Ultimately this theory will stand and fall according to its ability to show this connection, and the examples I have given are an attempt to show that it passes this test rather well. If that means a theory of human nature which is, at least in part, speculative, then that's a small price to pay.

Species-being and controversies of interpretation

Chapter 12

Collective control

One of the things that distinguished Marx from many of those who came before him was his belief that alienation was a state of affairs that could be overcome. Furthermore, it could only be overcome through a radical reorganisation of society. This meant a radical reassertion of control over production. Since alienation is rooted in the different ways in which societies organise social production, the solution lies in *re*-organising that production.

Primarily, this means abolishing the arrangement whereby labour is sold as a commodity. This requires abolishing the division of society into one class which has to sell its labour and another which buys it. Furthermore, this can only be achieved by a radical extension of democracy into the sphere of work. Under capitalism there is a great deal of rhetoric about democracy and freedom, yet democracy in the workplace is mostly non-existent. To overcome alienation, to organise production in a way that can be considered genuinely fulfilling and meaningful, it must be possible for workers to have a far more direct say in their labour.

This requires decision-making regarding the conditions of work to be in the hands of those who work, not those who own the workplace, or a tiny minority of appointed managers. It requires the creation of democratic structures within workplaces capable of making these decisions. It requires thinking about jobs and roles that empower people to do this, and removing those that inhibit them.

One of the most pervasive myths of capitalism is that managers and capitalists are the people who know best how work should be organised. We are told that any attempt by workers to take control over the production process will lead to anarchy and inefficiency. What they need is a visionary boss to keep them in line. In capitalist terms, this is true. A company or industry controlled by its workers within capitalism would find it difficult to compete without a boss keeping them in line, investigating new ways of squeezing every last piece of value from their workers. This is in part because workers might make decisions based on their human needs— making work more bearable, for example—rather than being entirely directed by the needs of profit.

But more broadly, it is not true at all that capitalists know best. It is the people who actually *do the work* who know how best to do it. If workers gain real control over work they can organise it in ways which are beneficial both to themselves and to wider society. History is full of such examples. In Algeria, after they had kicked out French imperialism, workers began to take back control of abandoned farms and factories. One example from an olive oil factory shows the scale of this:

A hundred factory workers organised a committee, cleaned up the debris, repaired the machines, and began production with tons of raw materials diverted from settler companies. At one all-night meeting they decided that the first annual profits would be shared equally for four purposes: taxes, repairs and purchase of machinery, loans to local agricultural committees, and the remainder as bonuses for themselves. They declared their solidarity with their "brother workers on the farms" and planned to provide new jobs for seasonally unemployed farm workers by processing other crops during the off-season.[137]

Even more importantly than reorganising work, this involves *reclaiming* it. It involves workers making work feel meaningfully their own, rather than something hostile, belonging to someone else. It is something they have a say in, something they do for themselves, and for society, not for a bullying boss or distant shareholder.

Marx differed from many of his contemporaries and indeed some commentators today, in denying that it was necessary to go backwards. Some felt that to overcome the alienation that capitalism brought it was necessary to return to the forms of production associated with feudalism—small handicrafts and workshops and the like. Perhaps only in this way could people become more creatively engaged and fulfilled in their work. The way these thinkers saw it, how could mass factory-style production, in vast workplaces, be anything other than alienating?

Of course, Marx, and Marxists, would advocate the abolition of some of the worst aspects of alienated production. You would hope that the kinds of conditions described at Foxconn in the previous chapters would be intolerable in any socialist society. However, this does not mean that it is necessary to give up the vast productive powers that capitalist production involved. Marx believed it was possible to reorganise mass production in a way that was genuinely unalienated. In fact, the new kinds of workplaces and processes that capitalism brought about created new possibilities for unalienated labour that did not exist before.

Because capitalism concentrated workers together in certain locations, and necessarily involved more complicated forms of cooperation, it created new possibilities for solidarity and collective organisation. Older forms of work had been more isolating and individualistic, but capitalism had made the collective aspect of work even more clear.

This meant that the task of reasserting control over the labour process required radically new and higher forms of democracy and organisation, instead of a retreat into individualistic forms of production. Workers can only take back control of the labour process collectively. Capitalist production has become so integrated and concentrated that taking it back into workers' control necessarily requires collective forms. You cannot divide up a factory between the workers—you take the big cogs, I'll take the small ones, someone else gets the levers. If you want to continue to benefit from that production, you have to find democratic forms to bring it under control.

Engels described this in terms of "socialised production". Capitalism had made production social, while it had maintained an individualised method of exchange. The way things were produced was, in fact, collective and cooperative (albeit with no collective control), but the way things were distributed between people was entirely individualised. This contradiction was one of the sources of crisis within capitalism. Engels argued:

> This solution can only consist in the practical recognition of the social nature of the modern forces of production, and therefore in the harmonising with the socialised character of the means of production. And this can only come about by society openly and directly taking possession of the productive forces which have outgrown all control, except that of society as a whole.[138]

The productive forces that capitalism had unleashed could be brought under control, but only collectively.

Historically these demands have taken concrete form, and the most inspiring example is the Russian Revolution of October 1917. In the struggles of the Russian working class against both the Tsarist dictatorship and their capitalist bosses, new forms of political organisation had developed. These were the "soviets", factory committees which organised in the interests of workers. In 1917 Lenin and the Bolsheviks adopted the slogan of "All power to the soviets". This was an important part of their revolutionary strategy, but it also contained a demand for the retransfer of political power to workers in the workplace, for the radical extension of democracy into areas where it had previously not existed.

The Russian Revolution, in its early stages, involved an extraordinary democratisation of working life. In his study of a Moscow metal works Kevin Murphy writes how in the period immediately following the revolution workers wrestled with the practical question of workplace democracy:

> Factory committee resolutions were subordinate to factory-wide meetings, regularly attended by 500 to 800 workers, that decided such matters as the firing of workers and managers, aid to families of deceased workers, holiday schedules, and contributions.[139]

Before the destruction of the Civil War began to take its toll, "workers of the Moscow metal works approximated the Marxist ideal of a united, irrepressible social force",[140] and "workplace democracy extended to the shop level as workers repeatedly invoked the right to elect and instantly recall their representatives".[141]

Sadly, the later history of the Soviet Union also offers an important lesson for the analysis of alienation, albeit in a different way. As the Civil War took its toll, both in terms of loss of life and industrial destruction, the revolutionary process began to stall. This allowed the state bureaucracy to increasingly assert control over society, forming a new dominant class. State control took the place of genuine democratic control, and the structures of capitalism were re-created, albeit under state ownership.

Some argued that the fact that industry was state-owned rather than owned by individual capitalists meant that alienation in the Soviet Union was not an issue. State-owned industries were in the hands of "the people", and thus not based on the various forms of alienation I described above. However, this was based on a (usually deliberate) confusion of collective control and state control. As long as the state itself remained a body set above the majority of people, over which they had little control, alienation persisted. People still had no say in how their working day was organised.

The persistence of alienation in the Soviet Union was important for many who attempted to develop a criticism of Stalinism. With the suppression of uprisings by Soviet tanks in Hungary in 1956 and Czechoslovakia in 1968 many in the West became disillusioned with these regimes. They began to revive an independent tradition of Marxism, which often drew heavily on the notion of alienation in Marx's early writings. These ideas represented a clear reproach to what called itself "actually existing socialism". This also meant that the debates about interpretation I described in Chapter 10 often took on a politically charged character: it suited some people to be able to argue that the notion of alienation was part of a youthful idealism that Marx abandoned.

Despite the claims of Stalinist apologists and defenders of capitalism alike, Marx and Engels never confused state control with collective control. In the chapters above I describe how Marx saw the state as a form of alienation. The following passage from Engels sums up the issue:

> The modern state, no matter what its form, is essentially a capitalist machine—the state of the capitalists, the ideal personification of the total national capital. The more it proceeds to the taking over of productive forces, the more does it actually become the national capitalist, the more citizens does it exploit. The workers remain wage-workers—proletarians. The capitalist relation is not done away with.[142]

Collective control

Engels did argue that state control could "bring to a head" the issue of workers' control, and pose new questions to the capitalist system. However, it did not itself remove the essential relations of capitalism.

Because, for Marx, the state itself was a form of alienation, it could not be the driving force for overcoming alienation. Rather, alienation had to be overcome "from below". This reflected Marx's rejection of Feuerbach's vision of overcoming alienation through education. In rejecting this division Marx was rejecting any model which saw social transformation as being the result of a particular minority acting on behalf of the majority, of *giving* back control. What was important was the majority actively *taking* back control.

This indicates the importance of the *political* aspect of overcoming alienation, rather than just the economic aspect. Reorganising production could not take place without a political transformation, without a revolution. This is the subject of the final chapter.

Chapter 13

Revolution

While Marx's analysis of alienation does offer some pointers towards a different way of organising society, he famously avoided offering definite blueprints for a future world. Marx is often criticised for this failure to offer a concrete vision, but it is entirely deliberate. This is because he believed that the ways in which society will be organised in the future can only be fully realised by those who create the new society. Marx believed that the emancipation of the working class had to be the act of the working class themselves, and that it was not up to him to "write recipes for the cookshops of the future".[143]

Marx believed that from our existing, alienated position within society it was difficult for us to imagine in any detail the shape of an alternative. The way that capitalism alienates us from each other and from ourselves makes it easier for the ruling class to spread ideas which divide people. The idea that "greed is good", that people should only pursue their self-interest, finds fertile ground in alienated society. Secondly, the social relationships of society restrict how much we can imagine possible futures. Marx argued that "the phantoms formed in the brains of men are also, necessarily, sublimates of their material life-process".[144] The kinds of things we can imagine, here, within capitalism, are limited, often in ways we do not realise.

These kinds of influences, which are often referred to as ideological, can be seen in literature. Science fiction and fantasy novels are capable of imagining entirely new forms of technology, fantastic magic and creatures, but are often remarkably bad at imagining new social relations. Fantasy novels like *Lord of the Rings* end up describing societies which, while inhabited by elves, dwarves and hobbits, exist in social structures which closely resemble feudal Europe.

How can we move beyond this situation? One suggestion is provided by the influential anti-capitalist thinker John Holloway, who has written about the need for a revolt of "doing against labour" in which we "stop making capitalism". He argues that we should look to examples of unalienated labour in our everyday lives. The following passage is typical of Holloway's argument:

> I am a teacher and I produce labour powers for sale on the market, but at the same time I encourage my students to think critically about society. I am a nurse in a private hospital and produce profits for my employers, but at the same time I try to help my patients through some of the most difficult moments of their lives. I work on an assembly line in a car factory and every few seconds that I have free, my fingers are busy practising the chords that I'll be playing on my guitar tonight in the band... In all these cases there is a standing outside capitalist labour, a projection against and beyond my entrapment within abstract labour.[145]

However, the problem for Holloway's account is that these experiences are not free of alienation in one form or another. It is part of the claims of Marx's theory that alienation affects even our most personal relationships. It seems unlikely, for example, that the car worker's relationship to his other band members will not be characterised by a certain degree of alienation.

Holloway's analysis is based on Marx's argument that all labour within capitalism can be understood as both concrete and abstract labour. Holloway identifies concrete labour with

Alienation

unalienated labour and abstract labour with alienated labour, arguing that therefore all human labour has an unalienated aspect (for Holloway "concrete labour" is simply the mature Marx's name for unalienated creative activity).

This is a misunderstanding—concrete labour is not the same thing as unalienated labour. For Marx, labour under capitalism produces commodities which have both a use-value and an exchange-value; concrete labour is labour understood as a producer of use-values, abstract labour as the producer of exchange-values. Capitalism requires both. Abstract labour would be of no use to capitalism at all if it wasn't abstracted *from* labour which produced use-values. However, there is nothing inherently unalienated about the production of a use-value. Bombs and Botox have use-values in capitalist society, and wouldn't be produced if they didn't, but their production and use doesn't seem to point towards unalienated possibilities. Concrete labour may always accompany abstract labour, but unalienated labour does not similarly accompany alienated labour.

Marx's solution to this problem lay in the need for revolution. For Marx revolution was necessary for two reasons:

> Both for the production on a mass scale of this communist consciousness, and for the success of the cause itself, the alteration of men on a mass scale is necessary, an alteration which can only take place in a practical movement, a revolution; the revolution is necessary, therefore, not only because the ruling class cannot be overthrown in any other way, but also because the class overthrowing it can only in a revolution succeed in ridding itself of all the muck of ages and become fitted to found society anew.[146]

The important emphasis here is on the *transformative* aspects of revolution. Through actively transforming society people also transform themselves and their outlooks.

Revolution is, for Marx, an essential part of overcoming alienation. It is through collectively taking action to transform society that people can begin to see the possibilities that alienation denied them. It is through the struggle of ordinary people against their oppression and exploitation that the possibility of a different way of organising human labour is created. This reflected a great confidence in the power of ordinary people to transform their lives, but it was not merely a matter of faith. Marx saw time and time again the extent to which class struggle opened up new possibilities for political change. The Silesian weavers mentioned in Chapter 3 were an early example, but even more significant for Marx was the Paris Commune of 1871.

In 1871, in the aftermath of French defeat in the Franco-Prussian War, working people in Paris rose up in revolt. They declared an independent commune, and began to entirely reorganise society. The significance of the commune for Marx was that it was "the political form at last discovered under which to work out the economical emancipation of labour".[147] Under the commune, "with labour emancipated, every man becomes a working man, and productive labour ceases to be a class attribute".[148] The commune confirmed, for Marx, both of his claims for the importance of revolution. Firstly, it showed its transforming potential:

The working class do not expect miracles from the commune. They have no ready-made utopias to introduce. They know that in order to work out their own emancipation, and along with it that higher form to which present society is irresistibly tending by its own economic agencies, they will have to pass through long struggles, through a series of historic processes, transforming circumstances and men.[149]

Secondly, the commune showed that the ruling classes would not give up without a fight. Sadly, the French state

Alienation

returned to crush the commune, and dash the hopes of all those in it in the most brutal way.

History is full of examples of the way that this kind of revolutionary activity involves challenging and overcoming alienation collectively. In the early 1980s a wave of strikes and workplace occupations led by the independent trade union Solidarity began to challenge repressive rule in Poland. During one such strike wave, a Communist Party newspaper carried a report from a hospital doctor. All of her working class patients had discharged themselves from hospital so as to join the workers' movement. In collectively organising to challenge their alienation they had actually come to feel better![150]

The way that revolution can transform people's horizons has also been clear in the recent uprisings in the Middle East and North Africa. What began as protests against repressive regimes have transformed into wider transformations of society, especially in Egypt. Sameh Naguib describes how being in Tahrir Square started to melt away old prejudices and divisions:

> The space in Tahrir was not simply occupied physically but spiritually. Harassment against women disappeared, tensions between Copts and Muslims evaporated. People shared food, water, cigarettes. Songs, music, poetry and chants filled the air. A new Egypt was being created.[151]

This was not just temporary elation on a mass demonstration, but the beginnings of a process which, as Marx put it, transforms circumstances and men. Demands for democracy constantly fuse with demands for economic transformation, and in turn these economic demands pose new political questions of how to organise society. Naguib continues:

> Freedom for the worker did not only mean freedom to vote or freedom of expression, it also meant freedom from

hunger, insecurity and the constant threat of unemployment... Dignity was a meaningless notion unless it meant an end to poverty and need.[152]

It is revolutions like the one in Egypt that give the most hope for the possibility of ending both the capitalist system and the alienation it brings with it. The revolution in Egypt may be the tip of the iceberg, where a process of people transforming both themselves and their surroundings can continue into a far more radical transformation. Or it may not. But it lights a beacon, indicating possibilities for the overwhelming majority to take back control of their lives, their work and their future, and in so doing build a better world.

Further reading

All of Marx's and Engels's works are available online at the excellent Marxists Internet Archive, www.marxists.org. Marx's most detailed writings on alienation are in his 1844 *Economic and Philosophical Manuscripts* (sometimes called the *Paris Manuscripts*), but references to alienation and connected concepts return throughout his work.

The two best books on alienation are Bertell Ollman's *Alienation: Marx's Concept of Man in Capitalist Society* and István Mészáros's *Marx's Theory of Alienation*. Both are significantly more complex than this book, but make rewarding reading. Sean Sayers' more recent book *Marx and Alienation* offers a very accessible account of the influence of Hegel and Marx, and engages well with some of the questions I address in Chapter 10.

Georg Lukács's work *History and Class Consciousness*, while hard going, offers a number of important insights into the connection between Marx's and Hegel's works. The chapter entitled "Reification and the consciousness of the proletariat" is an important contribution to understanding the connection between commodity fetishism and alienation.

Isaak Rubin's book *Essays on Marx's Theory of Value* contains an excellent account of commodity fetishism and also includes an excellent introduction by Fredy Perlman. Joseph Choonara's *Unravelling Capitalism* is an accessible introduction to Marx's economic theory.

Martin Empson's pamphlet *Marxism and Ecology* offers an excellent introduction to Marx's ideas about nature and environment. John Bellamy Foster's book *Marx's Ecology* offers the most detailed analysis of Marx's notion of metabolism and metabolic rift.

Kevin Doogan's book *New Capitalism* is an excellent reply to those who argue that work has changed in certain important ways. Paul Thompson's article "Foundation and Empire: A Critique of Hardt and Negri", in *Capital and Class* 86, deals more directly with Hardt and Negri's arguments.

A number of articles have made far more detailed attempts to connect the arguments about health inequality with theories of alienation than I have been able to here: Mike Haynes, "Capitalism, class, health and medicine", in *International Socialism* 123, and Ian Crinson and Chris Yuill, "What can alienation theory contribute to an understanding of social inequalities in health?", in *International Journal of Health Services* 38, are good examples. Iain Ferguson's interview with Richard Pickett in *International Socialism* 127 also raises these issues. For an impressive Marxist account of psychiatry and mental health issues see Peter Sedgwick's *Psychopolitics*.

Finally, *Ours to Master and to Own*, edited by Immanuel Ness and Dario Azzellini, draws together accounts and lessons from the history of workers' control throughout the history of capitalism, and makes inspiring and essential reading.

Notes

A note on references

All of Marx and Engels' works are freely available online at the Marxists Internet Archive. References to their works here are given by title and date and can be accessed at www.marxists.org

1   Jimmy Reid, "Rectorial Address", 1972, http://www.independent.co.uk/news/uk/politics/still-irresistible-a-workingclass-heros-finest-speech-2051285.html

2   As above.

3   *Socialist Worker*, 13 August 2011, http://www.socialistworker.co.uk/art.php?id=25681

4   *BBC News*, 9 August 2011, http://www.bbc.co.uk/news/uk-14458424

5   Bertell Ollman, *Alienation: Marx's Conception of Man in Capitalist Society* (Cambridge, 1977), p131.

6   Karl Marx, *A Contribution to the Critique of Hegel's Philosophy of Right* (1844).

7   Adam Smith, *The Wealth of Nations* (1776), http://www.econlib.org/library/Smith/smWN.html

8   Quoted in István Mészáros, *Marx's Theory of Alienation* (Merlin, 1970), p34.

9   Marx, *On the Jewish Question* (1844).

10 Jean-Jacques Rousseau, *Discourse on the Origin of Inequality* (1754), http://www.constitution.org/jjr/ineq.htm

11 Jean-Jacques Rousseau, *Discourse on the Arts and Sciences* (1750), http://records.viu.ca/~johnstoi/rousseau/firstdiscourse.htm

12 As above.

13 Jean-Jacques Rousseau, *The Social Contract* (1762), http://www.constitution.org/jjr/socon.htm.

14 As above.

15 Jean-Jacques Rousseau, *A Discourse on Political Economy* (1755), http://www.constitution.org/jjr/polecon.htm.

16 Charles Taylor, *Hegel* (Cambridge, 1975), p17.

17 GWF Hegel, *Phenomenology of Spirit* (1807), http://www.marxists.org/reference/archive/hegel/works/ph/phconten.htm

18 Friedrich Engels, *Ludwig Feuerbach and the End of Classical German Philosophy* (1886).

19 Marx, *Economic and Philosophical Manuscripts* (1844).

20 Marx, *Grundrisse* (1857).

21 Marx and Engels, *The German Ideology* (1846).

22 Marx, *Theses on Feuerbach* (1845).

23 As above.

24 As above.

25 Marx and Engels, *The Holy Family* (1845).

26 Marx, *Capital* Vol 1 (1867)

27 As above.

28 Engels, *Condition of the Working Class in England* (1844).

29 Marx, *A Contribution to the Critique of Hegel's Philosophy of Right* (1844).

30 As above.

31 Marx, *Critical Notes on the King of Prussia and Social Reform* (1844).

32 As above.

33 Marx and Engels, *The Communist Manifesto* (1848).

34 Alexis de Tocqueville, *Recollections of the French Revolution of 1848* (Transaction, 1987), p75.

35 Marx and Engels, *The Communist Manifesto* (1848).

36 Marx, *A Contribution to the Critique of Hegel's Philosophy of Right* (1844).

37 Marx, *Economic and Philosophical Manuscripts* (1844).

38 Marx, *Capital* Vol 1 (1867).

39 Marx, *Economic and Philosophical Manuscripts* (1844).

40 Marx, *Capital* Vol 1 (1867).

41 Marx, *Economic and Philosophical Manuscripts* (1844).

42 As above.

43 Marx, *Capital* Vol 1 (1867).

44 Marx, *Economic and Philosophical Manuscripts* (1844).

45 Marx, *Capital* Vol 1 (1867).

46 Alex Callinicos, *Universities in a Neo-Liberal World* (Bookmarks, 2005), p17.

47 Marx, *Grundrisse* (1857).

48 As above.

49 See EP Thompson, "Time, Work-Discipline, and Industrial Capitalism", *Past and Present* 38 (1967), pp56-97.

50 Chris Warhurst et al (eds), *Work Less, Live More?* (Palgrave MacMillan, 2008), p198.

51 As above, p204.

52 Georg Lukács, *History and Class Consciousness* (Merlin, 1971), p89.

53 Paul Stewart et al, *We Sell Our Time No More: Workers' Struggles Against Lean Production in the British Car Industry* (Pluto, 2009), p178.

54 As above.

55 Marx, *Economic and Philosophical Manuscripts* (1844).

56 As above.

57 As above.

58 Ben Hamper, *Rivethead: Tales from the Assembly Line* (Warner Books, 1992), p113.

59 As above, p160.

60 Marx, *Capital* Vol 1 (1867).

61 Emile Zola, *Germinal* (JM Dent, 1951), p9.

62 Paul Mason, *Live Working or Die Fighting* (Harvill Secker, 2007), pp53-54.

63 Marx, *Economic and Philosophical Manuscripts* (1844).

Notes

64 Marx and Engels, *The Communist Manifesto* (1848).

65 Marx, *Capital* Vol 3 (1863-1883).

66 Marx, *Capital* Vol 1 (1867).

67 As above.

68 As above.

69 Naomi Klein, *No Logo* (Picador, 2000), p370.

70 Marx, *Capital* Vol 1 (1867).

71 As above.

72 As above.

73 As above.

74 As above.

75 As above.

76 See Sheila McGregor, "Sexuality, Alienation and Capitalism", *International Socialism* 130 (Spring 2011), p185.

77 As above, p187.

78 Marx, *Economic and Philosophical Manuscripts* (1844).

79 Mészáros, as above, p82.

80 As above, p83.

81 Marx, *Economic and Philosophical Manuscripts* (1844).

82 As above.

83 As above.

84 Barbara Ehrenreich, *Nickel and Dimed* (Granta, 2002), p59.

85 Paul Stewart et al, as above, p128.

86 Jimmy Reid, as above.

87 *The Guardian*, 5 March 2010.

88 Marx, *The Civil War In France* (1871).

89 Marx and Engels, *The German Ideology* (1846).

90 Marx, *Grundrisse* (1857).

91 Bertell Ollman, as above, p156.

92 Marx, *Economic and Philosophical Manuscripts* (1844).

93 See Tony Lane and Kenneth Roberts, *Strike at Pilkingtons* (Fontana, 1971), p45.

94 http://www.telegraph.co.uk/finance/china-business/7773011/A-look-inside-the-Foxconn-suicide-factory.html

95 See Chris Warhurst et al (eds), *Work Less, Live More?*, as above, p203.

96 Paul Stewart et al, as above, p225.

97 Paul Thompson and Chris Warhurst, *Workplaces of the Future* (MacMillan, 1998), p181.

98 As above, pp180-181.

99 See Michael Marmot, "Social Differentials in Health Within and Between Populations", *Daedalus* 123 (4) (1994); Mike Haynes, "Capitalism, Class, Health and Medicine", *International Socialism* 123 (Summer 2009).

100 Richard Wilkinson and Kate Pickett, *The Spirit Level* (Penguin, 2009), p256.

101 See Michael Marmot et al, "Low Job Control and Risk of Coronary Heart Disease in Whitehall ii (prospective cohort) Study", *BMJ* 314 (1997), http://www.bmj.com/content/314/7080/558.full

102 Colin Sparks, "The Big Brother Phenomenon", *International Socialism* 114 (Spring 2007), p184.

103 Gavan MacCormack, *Client State* (Verso, 2007), p43.

104 Jacinta Tan et al, "Competence to make treatment decisions in anorexia nervosa: thinking processes and values", *Philos Psychiatr Psychol* 13(4) (2006), pp8-12.

105 LSE, Centre for Economic Performance, Mental Health Policy Group, *The depression report: a new deal for depression and anxiety disorders* (2006), http://eprints.lse.ac.uk/818/

106 See Peter Sedgwick, *Psychopolitics* (Pluto, 1982).

107 Martin Empson, *Marxism and Ecology* (Socialist Worker, 2009), p4.

108 Marx, *Economic and Philosophical Manuscripts* (1844).

109 Marx, *Capital* Vol 1 (1867).

110 Engels, *The Housing Question* (1872).

111 As above.

112 Marx, *Capital* Vol 1 (1867).

113 John Bellamy Foster, *Marx's Ecology* (Monthly Review Press, 2000), p158.

114 Engels, *Anti-Dühring* (1877).

115 Marx, *Capital* Vol 3 (1863-1883).

116 ONS, *Social Trends* 40 (Palgrave MacMillan, 2010).

117 As above.

118 Michael Hardt and Antonio Negri, *Empire* (Harvard, 2000), p280.

119 As above, p289.

120 As above, p294.

121 *New Statesman*, 28 May 2001.

122 Asaf Darr and Chris Warhurst, "Assumptions, Assertions and the Need for Evidence", *Current Sociology* 56 (2008), p73.

123 As above, p38.

124 Chris Warhurst et al (eds), *The Skills That Matter* (Palgrave MacMillan, 2004), Table 9.5.

125 As above, Table 9.6.

126 As above, p166.

127 Paul Thompson and Chris Warhurst, *Workplaces of the Future*, as above, p175.

128 As above, p204.

129 As above, p54.

130 As above, p53.

131 As above, p47.

132 As above, p41.

133 Iain Ferguson and Michael Lavalette, "Beyond Power Discourse: Alienation and Social Work", *British Journal of Social Work* 34 (2004), p304.

134 Kevin Doogan, *New Capitalism? The Transformation of Work* (Polity, 2009).

135 Martin Smith, "The Shape of the Working Class", *International Socialism* 113 (Winter 2007), p55.

136 István Mészáros, as above, p227.

137 See Immanuel Ness and Dario Azzellini, *Ours to Master and to Own* (Haymarket, 2011), p235.

138 Engels, *Socialism: Utopian and Scientific* (1880).

139 Kevin Murphy, *Revolution and Counterrevolution: Class Struggle in a Moscow Metal Factory* (Haymarket, 2005), p65.

140 As above, p73.

141 As above, p68.

142 Engels, *Socialism: Utopian and Scientific* (1880).

143 Marx, *Capital* Vol 1 (1867).

144 Marx and Engels, *The German Ideology* (1846).

145 John Holloway, *Crack Capitalism* (Pluto, 2010), p97.

146 Marx and Engels, *The German Ideology* (1846).

147 Marx, *The Civil War In France* (1871).

148 As above.

149 As above.

150 See Colin Barker and Kara Weber, "Solidarnosc: From Gdansk to Military Repression", *International Socialism* 15 (Winter 1982), p148n.

151 Sameh Naguib, *The Egyptian Revolution* (Bookmarks, 2011), p19.

152 As above, p37.